Pray Up Your Life

Pray Up Your Life

50 Powerful Prayer Practices to Help You
Create the Life You Desire

Charline E. Manuel

BALBOA.
PRESS

A DIVISION OF HAY HOUSE

First printing 2006
Revised by the author 2011

Scripture versions cited in this book are identified in Scripture Notes section of the book.

ISBN: 978-1-4525-4799-2 (sc)
ISBN: 978-1-4525-4798-5 (e)
ISBN: 978-1-4525-4797-8 (hc)

Library of Congress Control Number: 2012903646
Balboa Press books may be ordered through booksellers or by contacting:

Balboa Press
A Division of Hay House
1663 Liberty Drive
Bloomington, IN 47403
www.balboapress.com
1-(877) 407-4847

Printed in the United States of America

Balboa Press rev. date:4/5/2012

In loving memory of my mother, who modeled
for me the importance of prayer.

Table of Contents

**Prayer Practices That Move You Forward
for New Opportunities**

How to Use This Book

This book may be read from beginning to end in sequence. However, because of the subject matter, you may be guided to read a chapter that addresses some current interest in your life. Many of the prayer practices in this book are related and complement each other. If you do decide to read this book out of sequence, you may want to consider first glancing through some of the chapters to see how you may combine prayer practices for greater effect.

Each chapter opens with a scripture I call the "Prayer Anchor" for that particular lesson. It reveals the theme and the background for the particular prayer practice listed. Each chapter ends with what I call "Prayer Practice," which describes how to put the lesson into practical use in your life.

Prayer, as I use it throughout the book, is conscious, intentional communion with God. Sometimes we pray aloud, and at other times we may pray silently. When we pray aloud, we focus our attention inward and speak life-affirming words that heal, bless, prosper, and celebrate God working in and through us. We use our words to voice the good that we desire for ourselves and others. Words are powerful, so we direct our prayers by carefully choosing the words we speak, whether in conscious communion with God or in conversation with others.

When we pray silently, our attention is also directed inward; we concentrate on spiritual ideals that allow us to fix our thoughts on truth. We concentrate on divine love, life, wisdom, peace, wholeness, order, and faith in God as all good. The more time we spend in prayer, the greater our ability to experience God as the loving presence within us. *Pray Up Your Life* supplies fifty powerful ways to help you consciously pray all the time and for every purpose.

In many of the prayer practices, I suggest a certain number of times or days to work with a particular method. I believe, as did the ancients regarding the use of numbers. As we read the Bible and other sacred texts, it is clear that in ancient times, numbers had implications beyond their numerical value. For example, the number 7 is used more than any other number in the Bible. It is no surprise that seven was believed to be the most sacred of all numbers.

Other numbers in the scriptures were also used to denote the deeper significance of mental, emotional and spiritual internal conditions. For example, a period of forty days represented deep spiritual times for Moses, Elijah, and Jesus. Surely the writers of the scriptures wanted to draw attention to the spiritual work completed during those forty days.

We also see the numbers 3 and 12 used frequently. In the science of numbers, called numerology, it is revealed that each number has a meaning, a purpose, and a message. I use the number 9 several times in the prayer practices, as it is the number 3 (the number representing the Trinity in Christian thought) multiplied by itself and for this reason is used to denote higher spiritual work. Also, nine is the highest of the series of the single digits 1 through 9 and therefore known as the number of endings and completion.

I first became interested in the significance of numbers as used in the scriptures many years ago when I had a revealing dream. I had been going through a challenging time and went to bed one night in tears crying out to God for guidance about what I should do about a particular situation that seemed overwhelming. In the dream, I saw myself celebrating that the situation had been cleared up, and I was telling other people that my problem had been solved after forty days. Then, while still dreaming, I heard, "Pray for forty days, and the answer will come."

When I woke up, I wrote the dream in my journal so as not to forget the details. I did as was instructed in the dream. I took my calendar and numbered it forty days out. I prayed daily about my request for guidance, and on the fortieth day, the answer was so clear that I was at first amazed and then curious. Why forty? It was then that my personal study of the science of numbers began, not to mention my interest in the study of dreams. It took several years before I understood that the change needed for my prayer to be answered was me, and that inner shift took forty days of consistent prayer.

When I make suggestions regarding the number of repetition for specific prayer practices, it is to support the inner change that leads to answered prayer. Generally, numbers 3 and 7 are used for creating new ideas, planting and growing seeds for new opportunities; 9 is used where higher spiritual work is required or to bring something to a harmonious conclusion, or orderly ending—which sets the stage for new beginnings; 12 gives added power to an idea; 40 is for situations where deep inner work is required.

If you find this interesting, I would suggest doing some further study of numerology. I have included a bibliography to help you find more information on topics discussed in this book. You may also want to do some additional reading of the scriptures that specifically list numbers and study the context in which those numbers are used.

For now, I invite you to be conscious of numbers that seem to be prevalent in your life. Most people have what they call a lucky number. I do not subscribe to the idea of luck but would say that certain numbers do have positive meaning in our lives. Unless you are guided otherwise, use the numbers I suggest or numbers that you feel pulled toward. The idea is for you to have a guide. I also suggest you customize these prayer practices as you are guided.

In *Pray Up Your Life*, you will find discussion on outer symbols to enhance your prayer experience. Keep a balance between the outer symbols and your inner work. I cannot stress enough that our work is always internal; the outer symbols can help to enhance the experience, but please remember that God is our source, and we connect with God by going within ourselves. As you read through the chapters, you will find God referred to by other titles such as Spirit, Creator, and Higher Power.

God answers prayers! You have in your hands tools to help you demonstrate the good that you desire. However, it is my premise throughout *Pray Up Your Life* that God answers our prayers according to our dominant thoughts, feelings, beliefs, and words that we speak. As you work with the various prayer methods in *Pray Up Your Life*, you will condition your mind for the good that you desire; a mind conditioned for good is a magnet for great, grand, and awesome experiences to manifest.

God does indeed answer prayers. However, God answers our prayers according to our receptive state of mind, the level of faith in our hearts, our willingness to cooperate with divine order, and the power of the Holy Spirit that is active on our behalf as grace. The prayer practices in this book are not quick fixes for life's challenges; they are steady, time-tested, Bible-based approaches to support the conscious awareness of God's presence within us. Implement the prayer practices that speak to you, knowing that God, in you, cannot and will not fail.

Introduction

This book is titled as a true story. That is to say, the spiritual practices in this book have blessed my life in countless ways. So when I say that what you have here are "fifty powerful prayer practices," I mean just that. I offer them to you because I know that for the person who is sincere about wanting to grow spiritually and is willing to put prayer into practice in his or her life, the growth, expansion of consciousness, answers, and revelations desired will surely come.

As you engage in the ideas in this book, you will "pray up" your life with thoughts, words, and actions that reveal God's grace being active within and all around you. As you invest time and energy using these and other prayer practices, you will create the life that you desire.

There are as many ways to pray as there are people on the planet. Prayer is a personal experience. Quite frankly, I don't think we need another book on "how to pray." There is sufficient material already in print to teach the basic mechanics of prayer. Yes, some are more detailed than others, and each has its own particular approach largely depending on the religious or spiritual views of the author.

Yet I've discovered there are times along life's journey that we feel the need to vary our prayer methods to address specific desires we may have. Let's face it—there are times in our lives when "stuff" is happening, and we seek something more to help us prayerfully move through the experience. So this book is written not to teach how to pray but to complement your prayer life in general.

When you use the prayer practices in this book,

- you'll add a variety of practical, effective methods by which to confirm God's presence within you;

- you'll be reminded that there is no one right way to become aware of the power of God in your life;

- you'll discover techniques to assist you in developing a prayer consciousness that will result in a life of prayer;

- you'll know what it is to "pray without ceasing"; and

- you'll consciously be in action to create the life you desire to enjoy.

There is another benefit to putting these and other prayer practices to work in your life. The more time we spend consciously in prayer, we "pray up" the life we desire for ourselves. I use an investment analogy when I think of praying up our lives. We invest money in a bank account so that we always have money available to meet our needs. When we pray up our lives, we invest positive, life-affirming, uplifting, truth based thoughts and words into our consciousness. In this way, we build a strong, abundant spiritual bank account capable of supporting the desires of our hearts and working through the opportunities we will face in the future.

When we live a life that is prayed up, we joyfully move through our day-to-day experiences with confidence. We know that at all times we are able to draw on a consciousness grounded in the spiritual dominion of unwavering faith, steadfast love, and the blessed assurance of the power, strength, wisdom, and substance to meet our every need. To abide in this state of consciousness, I'm suggesting the tools offered in *Pray Up Your Life*.

I am among those who believe that every thought, word, and act is a form of prayer. I call this our "natural prayer state." We're communicating with God all the time, and while we can't change the fact that we're praying all the time, we can change *what* and *how* we are praying.

In *Pray Up Your Life*, I refer to prayer as "conscious, intentional communion with God." The more we pray in this fashion, the more we shape our natural prayer state. So this book reveals methods for how you may affect your natural prayer state—every thought, word, and act—by increasing your time, energy, and effort spent in conscious, intentional communion with God.

Each chapter of the book has a Bible scripture as its theme. You'll discover from reading the scriptures alone that there are a variety of methods for prayer for many different purposes. The scripture references provide the foundation from which many of the spiritual practices we use today originate. Certainly, we have evolved in spiritual consciousness from ancient times, but the innate yearning to know and experience God has not changed. No matter what technique or method we use, we want the same thing today that our ancestors wanted, and our avenue for achieving it remains the same: prayer.

Also, I wrote this book to address many questions I have received regarding prayer in my role as a minister. For example, I've been asked to perform house, car, and business blessings. I've been asked if it is okay to pray for money when the Bible says, "The love of money is the root of all evil." I've been asked what kinds of prayers someone can pray to attract a mate. I've been asked how we can best pray for our loved ones. I've been asked if it is okay to use outer symbols when praying, and if so how and if not, why not. I've been asked for suggestions to make prayers more powerful.

Sometimes we have particular prayer requests, and we want some sound guidance or suggestions on what to do and how to do it. This book reveals what I call prayer practices, or practical methods we may incorporate into our spiritual work to support specific areas of interest and concern in our lives.

During the twenty years before I wrote this book, I varied my own prayer methods, and as a result, I developed a deeper spiritual foundation and feeling of personal closeness with God. I am not suggesting that it is the method that improves our relationship with God, but our methods may support us in developing the habit of conscious, consistent communion with God. When our connection with God is strengthened, our faith and trust in God deepens. This deeper relationship enhances the outcomes of our prayers.

The various methods in this book helped me discover that God is my source of all good. I discovered that regardless of the methods I use, I must at least abide by spiritual principles and consciously put them into living practice until they become a way of life. By these and various other methods, I found great meaning in the words, "...the kingdom of God is within you" (Luke 17:21 NKJV).

Each person has his or her own understanding of what prayer is and how to pray. Most of us learned about prayer during childhood. Many of us continue with those same beliefs, and they shape our current prayer habits. Unless we delve deeper into ourselves or study prayer, we generally keep the same habits that we've always had.

For example, when I was a child, my mother had us kneel before the bed at night to pray. Mostly we said, "Now I lay me down to sleep, I pray the Lord my soul to keep, if I should die before I wake, I pray the Lord my soul to take." We could then add "God bless" and name all the members of our family and any friends we wanted to include, and that was it.

Well, as soon as I was an adult, I dropped that cute little prayer; I didn't like the part "if I should die before I wake." I just didn't want to go to sleep at night thinking about dying. However, for many years I continued the practice of kneeling before my bed to pray, and sometimes I do indeed kneel when I pray but not with the belief that this is the only method of saying my nightly prayer. I have discovered that kneeling is not the only way to humble myself in communion with God. Since then, I have given myself permission to use other methods of praying and humbling my ego to surrender in sweet communion with the God of my being.

This book is written primarily from my own varied experiences with prayer. I've tried every practice in this book, and each one revealed answers and provided results. But I must caution you: the answers and results were not always as I had hoped or what I had anticipated. However, I developed a wider trust and appreciation for what prayer truly is to me, and it is my constant effort to know and experience God as a living power within me. So when I say "the God of my being" I'm referring to the personal relationship I have developed with my Creator through living a life of prayer. Let the outcome of your prayers be the unfolding of God's highest good for your life. The prayer practices herein lend themselves to an open heart and a willing mind ready to be guided by God's plan of absolute good.

This book is about giving yourself permission to pray in whatever way feels right for you and that is in alignment with your beliefs and understanding of truth. Feel free to put your own variation to the prayer practices so that they feel customized for you. Be willing to let the results and answers help you grow. Let the works revealed to you help you grow. Isn't that why we pray—so that we may grow into the full realization of all that God created us to be?

With each prayer practice in *Pray Up Your Life*, may you experience the presence of God as your holy self. May you feel the grace and beauty of being fully alive in the sacred chasm of unlimited possibilities. May every prayer find gratitude on your lips, love in your heart, and celebration in your soul.

Part 1

Prayer Practices That Cover the Basics

1

First Things First

Prayer Anchor: "In the beginning God
created the heavens and the earth."

Genesis 1:1 (NKJV)

When we make a conscious intention to pray, it is best to start at the beginning. In the book of Genesis, where the allegorical account of creation is told, a great wisdom is revealed that we can use for our benefit. It unveils the importance of having a conscious place to start. One way to look at this is that the Genesis narrative says God started the creation process *at* the beginning. Another way to see it is that God *is* the beginning. From either perspective, whatever we plan to create or to do, the best place to start is with God at the beginning.

When we affirm "In the beginning God" in prayer, we are setting an intention to co-create with God the desires of our heart. We are positioning ourselves at the point where the creative process begins—with God. We are in effect, saying something like, God is the beginning, God started at the beginning, and that's where I will start too—with God as the beginning."

This principle of starting at a specific place called the beginning can be referred to as "first things first." We see this idea modeled for us in nature. The farmer must prepare the soil first before planting his seeds in the ground. To bypass this important step would surely affect the quality and quantity of his crops. His harvest would not bring forth the crop that he desired because he did not honor the rule of first things first.

In spiritual matters, we follow this principle by acknowledging God first. "But seek first the kingdom of God and His righteousness, and all these things shall be added to you."[1]

When we acknowledge God as the foundation on which we pray, we are open and receptive to receive God's direction to the right and perfect answers. This affirms that we want God to be at the core of the outcome. In this way, we make a conscious decision to surrender our personal will to the will of God and therefore to humble ourselves in prayer. Without a little humility, we might make the error that so many folks make, and that is to think that we—apart from God—can achieve the desires of our hearts.

We would do well to remember, "Trust in the Lord with all your heart, And lean not on your own understanding; In all your ways acknowledge Him, And He shall direct your paths."[2] "In the beginning God" invites God into our prayers and acknowledges that we know that we need and want divine guidance and assistance.

If we go back and read the creation story, we will see that great patience was taken one day at a time, step by step, to create heaven and earth, living creatures, and humankind. And God did not stop until the job was done. Our Creator does not begin something only to later abandon it—or us. God will see it through to completion in us, according to our willingness to follow the steps, stay open to the process, and start with God at the beginning.

"Then God saw everything that He had made, and indeed it was very good."[3] So the story goes that after the work was done, God found it favorable and then rested. This is the process we want to follow: We begin with God, follow the steps with great care and patience, trust that the creative process is sound and creates according to a divine plan, know that it will be completed in divine order, and then rest in the realization that it is very good.

God started at the beginning, took the process through to completion, and was pleased with the results. Isn't that what you want; to start at the beginning, stay the course through completion, and then end up with an outcome where you may affirm it is very good? Our first prayer practice invites you to engage the creative process, beginning with God.

Prayer Practice

In your time of daily prayer, begin by acknowledging God's presence. Establish from the start that you are consciously aware that God is the foundation of your life and the source of all that you are, all that you desire to be, have, and experience. God first!

As you become consciously aware of God's presence in prayer, turn your attention inward. When you experience God within you, you add great power to your prayer and your ability to follow through on the outcomes you receive. "… For indeed, the kingdom of God is within you."[4]

Here are a few statements you may use at the beginning of your prayer experience to acknowledge God. Select one or all. The idea is to pray from a consciousness that is grounded in the awareness of God. Say these aloud, concentrate on them, and meditate on them while turning your attention within. After you are centered in God's presence, you are ready to express your prayer desires.

- *"In the beginning, God"*. Fix the idea in your mind that you are one with God, starting out on a prayerful journey within.

- *"I now acknowledge the kingdom of God within me."* As you pray this statement, turn your attention within—focus on your heart, on your breathing, or toward your abdomen.

- *"God is. I am."* Repeat this statement until you feel a sense of peace and relaxation, knowing that you are one with God.

- *"I AM THAT I AM."* Repeat this over and over while your attention is on your breathing. Vary your emphasis from *"I AM THAT"* to *"I AM."* In the book of Exodus, one of the names for God is revealed to Moses. "And Moses said unto God, Behold, when I come unto the children of Israel, and shall say unto them, The God of your fathers hath sent me unto you; and they shall say to me, What is his name? what shall I say unto them? And God said unto Moses, I AM THAT I AM: and he said, Thus shalt thou say unto the children of Israel, I AM hath sent me unto you."[5]

- *"I am now consciously aware of God's presence within me."* Whenever you think or speak the words "I am," remember the scripture from Exodus 3:14. "I am" is your personal name for God—only you can say I am for you.

As you focus your attention on God within, you are engaging your higher self in a sacred meeting where the creative process is set in motion—the beginning. Be patient, and trust that God's carefully designed creative process works and will bring forth results for your prayer in powerful and awesome ways.

2

Pray and Get Ready

Prayer Anchor: "Therefore I say to you, whatever things you ask when you pray, believe that you receive them, and you will have them."

Mark 11:24 (NKJV)

Ask anyone who prays with a specific request in mind if he or she believes the prayer will be answered. Most will say, "Yes! I believe." However, our true beliefs reveal themselves in and through our actions. We can gauge the level of our belief in our answered prayer by noticing the consistency among our thoughts, words, and actions.

So often I have witnessed others praying for a particular need say, "Amen," then go right back to talking as if nothing has changed or will change. To pray and believe means that we consciously open ourselves in communion with God on a matter and then trust that our highest good will manifest. We second-guess neither the prayer nor the God who is able to deliver. We move forward, expecting that results will be realized. Next, we begin to act as though our prayer shall, indeed, be answered with the right and perfect God-directed outcome.

I once was acquainted with a young woman who prayed for male companionship. She prayed, made a treasure map (a prayer desire displayed in pictures), and asked others to pray with her. After several months of all this effort, a young man new to the church that we both attended asked her to accompany him to a work-related social function. I was shocked when she told me she declined the invitation. When I asked her why, she had a list of excuses. She had nothing to wear, she didn't feel comfortable with their first date being a large gathering, she didn't have time to get her hair done before the event, on and on and on. If she had believed her prayer would indeed manifest as she was praying all those months, she would have been preparing in every conceivable way to say yes to an opportunity when it did, indeed, arise.

For our prayers to be even more effective, we infuse thoughts and words that support an inner embrace of what we are praying about. In other words, our beliefs show up in our actions. If we truly believe that what we pray for can be ours and is ours, we will pray and refuse to let minor excuses become obstacles to the opportunities that arise as a result of our prayers.

The epilogue to the story above is that after the woman declined the young man's invitation, he asked another woman in the church to attend the event, and she said *yes*. They began dating and, two years later, were married.

Now, it is true that all is in divine order with regard to who ended up with whom. However, if we pray specifically for something we say we want, our job is to pray and prepare for the opportunities that will present themselves as possible answers to our prayer.

When we pray, we create and send forth an energy field that begins to work on our behalf. This young man may not have been "the one" for the first young woman, but his appearance in her life does suggest that she was sending out positive energy for what she was praying about. However, when we aren't prepared for a response to our prayer, we send forth a mixed signal regarding what we desire. In times like these, our demonstration may be delayed or redirected toward someone who is "ready" to receive the blessing.

If the young man was not of the particular liking that the first woman desired in a companion, it was proper that she redirect his advances. However, to reject his advances with trivial excuses (like not having anything to wear) speaks to being unprepared for the very thing for which she had been praying.

Great power is added to our prayer when we set in motion action in preparation for the good we desire.

Prayer Practice

Periodically check your level of belief. Take the prayer anchor for this chapter into your time of prayer and meditate on the words. Concentrate on its meaning to you. Determine if your outer actions are in alignment with what you are praying. Observe your thoughts, words, and actions to see if they do indeed reflect what you are praying. If not, this is an area you may decide to work on. If your thoughts and outer actions are in alignment with your prayer, begin immediately preparing for the demonstrations sure to be drawn to you.

Pray with your whole heart for what you desire to manifest in your life. Use the techniques in this book and others that you know. Whether you speak your prayers aloud, affirm them in the silence of your being, write them in your prayer journal, or pray them with your prayer group, when you act as though you believe the prayer is a living reality, you cooperate with the spirit of God within you to bring the prayer into manifestation.

Whenever our prayers are delayed, the first place to examine ourselves is in the area of belief. Your part in manifesting your desire is to pray, believe, and prepare for the demonstration you seek. If there is some particular desire you are praying to manifest, set it in your mind to do something daily in preparation for its manifestation. If your desire is really what you want, you'll know because you will enjoy preparing to receive it.

3

Stay Positive

<u>Prayer Anchor</u>: "Finally, beloved, whatever is true, whatever is honorable, whatever is just, whatever is pure, whatever is pleasing, whatever is commendable, if there is any excellence and if there is anything worthy of praise, think about these things."

Philippians 4:8 (NRSV)

Our power to decide what we will think, what we will say, and what we will do is truly one of God's greatest gifts. I can remember times in my life when I was firm on a decision that I had made, and with unwavering, persistent faith, miraculous things happened. I had set in mind an intention and made a decision, and my outer circumstances cooperated with my mental choice.

One such time was when I decided to go back to school to get my master's degree. I had just moved to Kansas City, Missouri, the previous year with my son, who was five years old at the time. I had no family there and knew only a few people I worked with and a few friends in my church family. The challenge was who would baby-sit Benjamin while I took classes at night. I remember thinking on the day I registered for classes, "I don't know how I'm going to do this without something in place for my son's care." But I registered anyway.

Until the night of my first class, I had no one to look after Benjamin. I fed him dinner, praying the whole time something like, "Dear God, I know I'm going to class tonight, and I know that Benjamin will be safely cared for—I just don't know how yet, but I know there is an answer." Even Benjamin was concerned. He must have asked ten times or more, "Where am I going when you go to school? Am I going with you? Who's going to keep me?"

Just after we had finished dinner, there was a knock at the door, and it was a little boy and his mom who lived a few buildings away in our apartment complex. Benjamin had played with the boy, and I knew his mother only well enough to say hello in passing and to wave to when the boys were playing. The boy and his mother came to invite Benjamin to their home that evening. It was the boy's birthday, and the mom was inviting a few of the neighborhood boys over for ice cream and cake and to play a few games. I told her I had to attend a class that night and would not be back until about 9 p.m. She said that was fine.

That was the start of what became a friendship with this woman who kept Benjamin when I had night classes. On Saturdays, when she needed to run errands, I kept her son with Benjamin and me. I could not have planned a better arrangement myself.

But that experience taught me the power of a made-up mind. I had decided I was going back to school, and the details were worked out beyond what I could have ever imagined. Staying positive can make the difference in achieving a seemingly challenging goal.

One tool for helping us to form our desires in our mind is focus. Focus can propel us toward our desires in miraculous ways. When we focus on what we want rather than what we do not want, we set in motion the power to manifest the desires of our heart. With the conscious, faithful, and persistent focus of our thoughts, we become magnets for unseen possibilities to find us. The process of affirmations (positive statements of truth) and denials (statements that drive negative thoughts from our mind) help us form the quality of thoughts that draw to us the good we desire.

So often it appears that our prayers are not answered, yet the truth may be that we were not clear, definite, or specific about what we were praying for in the first place. Affirmations and denials help us get into the mental space of knowing what we desire. Once the desire is clear in our mind, we anchor the desire with the steady flow of positive thoughts. Desire can take the form of a powerful energy when set in motion as a series of affirmations spoken aloud; this is called affirmative prayer. When we make positive thinking a habit, we prepare our minds for positive results.

Prayer Practice

The prayer anchor for this chapter can be helpful in training the mind to think positively. For nine days, write the scripture shown as the prayer anchor for this chapter as though you are writing a letter to yourself. Imagine your "higher self" writing this important message to you for your greater good. Write it out this way three times each of the nine days as early in the morning as you can: "*Finally, beloved_____ (your name), today, _____(day and date) set your mind on whatever is true, whatever is honorable, whatever is just, whatever is pure, whatever is pleasing, whatever is commendable. If there is any excellence and if there is anything worthy of praise, think about these things.*"

Each day, after you have written the letter, prayerfully read it in your own handwriting first aloud, the second time softly, and the third time, think it to yourself. Then spend a few minutes in silent concentration on this scripture.

This is a mind-conditioning prayer. It will help you form positive thinking as a habit and a way of approaching your life situations. If you do have a particular prayer request that you are working with and staying positive is a challenge for you, say the scripture as a prayer three times before you give your attention to your specific request.

Spend your days thinking about your affairs in the most positive way that you can. If you find yourself falling into negative thinking, recite the scripture to yourself a few times to get back on track. You'll be amazed at the difference this prayer practice can make in the overall quality of your life and affairs.

4

Be Persistent—Pray Until Something Happens

Prayer Anchor: "And he said to them, 'Suppose one of you has a friend, and you go to him at midnight and say to him, "Friend, lend me three loaves of bread; for a friend of mine has arrived, and I have nothing to set before him." And he answers from within, "Do not bother me; the door has already been locked, and my children are with me in bed; I cannot get up and give you anything." I tell you, even though he will not get up and give him anything because he is his friend, at least because of his persistence he will get up and give him whatever he needs.'"

Luke 11:5-8 (NRSV)

Jesus tells this parable as a lesson in persistence. If our desires are worth anything to us, then certainly they are worthy of our persistent attention and consistent efforts. If we set an intention to pray until something happens toward the manifestation of our prayer, if we persist, *something* will indeed happen.

Repetition or persistently affirming a particular prayer until it is satisfied is a technique that has been effective throughout the ages. Joshua had the children of Israel walk around the walls of Jericho seven times before it fell; Elijah had his servant looked for rain seven times before it rained. In Psalm 119, the psalmist says he praises God seven times each day. Daniel prayed three times a day.

First of all, you can never pray too much or too often. In fact, we are praying all the time in the normal course of our day; we just don't call it prayer. Every thought contributes to our overall prayer consciousness and therefore affects what we demonstrate as answered prayer.

So when you have a prayer for which you desire to see something specific manifest, persistent prayer can be the approach to take. In this prayer method, you are praying the same prayer until you see some results or until you feel a sense of total peace regarding your desire.

In the prayer anchor for this chapter, Jesus tells the story of a friend who knocks on a family's door at midnight. The family is already in bed, and the man of the house does not want to disturb the household by answering the door. But the friend knocks with great persistence. He needs help and will not let the family rest until he gets what he desires.

When we make a decision to pray until we get some results, we have the attitude of the friend who persisted at the door. Just as he knocked once and then twice and however many times it took to receive his desire, we, too, can use that same kind of perseverance to attain what we want. We can apply that same kind of strength of mind toward our desires until we feel the movement of Spirit on behalf of our prayer.

The key to repetition and persistence in our prayer desire is not to lose heart. We must be so grounded in our faith that we keep praying until we see, feel, and know that some change has and is occurring. Do not be easily discouraged. Do not give up if nothing appears to happen as soon as you think it should. "Then Jesus told them a parable about their need to pray always and not to lose heart."[1]

Remember that Spirit is at work, though you may not see the outer results immediately. Your part is to not give up. "But Jesus answered them, my Father is still working and I also am working."[2] As we pray persistently, with each time that we affirm our desire, we become increasingly assured of a blessed outcome.

In my spiritual community, we conduct an annual "pray until something happens" prayer vigil. Each person sets an intention toward specific desires, put them in writing, and commit to persistently pray for the prescribed time of the vigil, which is generally ninety to 120 days. The idea in this kind of exercise is to practice persistent, faithful repetition of our prayer desire, expecting something awesome as the result. It has always been a joy to hear the many expressions of gratitude for demonstrations made as a result of persistent prayer.

When we trust the spirit of God, giving our time, attention, faith, expectation, and persistent effort to our prayer, something must and will unfold. To set an intention and commitment to pray until something happens is a powerful process that can yield blessings beyond our imagination.

Prayer Practice

This prayer practice is about setting an intention to be persistent in your prayer work until you reach a state of personal fulfillment regarding your desire. Start by setting the number of days you will pray for your specific desire. Next, decide how many times each day and if you will use a specific prayer or format. These decisions will depend on your commitment and your level of desire.

If reading the prayer anchor daily helps keep you focused on persistent action, then by all means do so. Persistent, positive, faith-centered prayer is your work. To help you gain clarity regarding your prayer desire, write it out as clearly as possible. This will help clarify your desire and assure that you are praying the same prayer each time. Decide how long you are willing to stick with the prayer: until something happens within you or in your outer affairs, until some situation occurs that meets your need, or until the prayer desire moves in another direction.

The idea of praying until something happens is reaching the point when you feel complete and that the prayer is done. You may sense an inner readiness before the outer manifestation of it. Perhaps you will arrive at a mental state where you feel it is no longer desirous or necessary to pray the prayer. There can be a range of revelations besides having your desire met as requested, such as discovering that the prayer is no longer a desire, that your needs have changed over the course of the prayer, and/or that Spirit may have something better in store.

It is important to stay open to all possibilities. Your intention is that "something" will happen as a result of your persistent prayers. You will be most effective as you build an inner assurance that whatever does happen will be for your highest good.

Focus is important and a major help in staying persistent in your prayer efforts. I suggest using what I call a focus tool to help; this may be keeping a journal specifically for this prayer practice. With each day that you pray for your desire, you write something regarding its manifestation. For example, if your prayer desire is for a new car, you may write in your journal what you'll do when you have the car, places you'll go, people you see riding with you in the car, etc. You'll write about aspects of the desire that will be exciting, fun, and uplifting for you. Focus is the key to maintaining perseverance.

Set your intentions before you start this prayer practice. Put your energy into living out the intentions each day until you see a change, results, transformation, miracles, or some level of personal satisfaction as a result of your prayer. Prayer changes us, and the more we focus our time, energy, commitment, and faith in prayer, we can be assured that *something* can and will happen on our behalf, and we can rest assured it will be very good.

5

Practice Seeing

Prayer Anchor: "And the LORD said to Abram, after
Lot had separated from him: 'Lift your eyes now and look
from the place where you are—northward, southward,
eastward, and westward; for all the land which you
see I give to you and your descendants forever.'"

Genesis 13:14-15 (NKJV)

This wonderful scripture tells us that our Creator has made provisions for our needs to be met and, that with the use of our imagination we can claim them. Our constructive use of imagination is one way that we can help bring our good into manifestation. When we can use our imagination to envision whatever we desire we are cooperating with the idea expressed in the scripture *all that we can see, can be ours*. If you close your eyes right now, can you see the life you desire? Can you imagine your prayer request as already fulfilled? Do you have a vision of the things you desire to have? the person you desire to become?

When I was in elementary school, I was often labeled as a daydreamer. I sometimes would not finish my assignments because I would stare out the window dreaming of all kinds of experiences. I think one of my favorite things to do as a child was to stare out the window. I could do it for hours. By the time I reached high school, however, I had set aside my tendency to just sit and stare out the window and daydream. Little did I know as a child that I was developing my imagination and the powerful spiritual tool of visualization. The God-given ability we have to see things that are not visible to the human eye is the mighty power we have to imagine.

When you dream while you are asleep, you see pictures with your eyes closed. You may even see something in a dream before it actually happens. This confirms that the mind can and does have the ability to display pictures before they can be seen in the outer realm.

Little did I know as I was daydreaming that I was developing my ability to visualize and therefore give power to the manifestation of what I desired. When we think with specific pictures of an experience we'd like to have, we are using the powerful mental tool of daydreaming, visualizing, or picturing to utilize our imagination. It strengthens our conscious ability to hold a picture in mind. Once we impress on the conscious and subconscious levels of mind the picture of our desire, it's like posting it on the universal bulletin board—the announcement is made known in the vase sea of invisible ideas. The picture will then be irresistibly drawn to the one who has practiced seeing it.

Some folks have more difficulty using their imagination to see pictures in their mind. In this case, using outer pictures can be helpful to train the mind to see pictures inwardly. The idea is to look at pictures with your physical eyes until you can close your eyes and see the same picture in your mind and then begin to create pictures about whatever else you desire to manifest. What we see with feeling and strong desire, we can expect to draw to us.

Many of us are prone to daydreaming. Once we begin to understand this great power, we will not spend endless hours imagining what we do not wish to manifest in our lives. Rather, we will begin to practice seeing what we truly desire.

Some people have a strong ability to close their eyes and see things that have not yet manifested in the physical realm. Others must put more practice into being able to see ideas in their mind. Creative folks such as artists, designers, and architects have a more developed gift for seeing a picture in their mind and then putting it into a visible form for others to see. This technique, visualization, is something we can use to manifest the good that we desire.

Try this exercise: Find a picture that represents something you would like to have or experience. Look at the picture for a few minutes with admiration and desire. Now, imagine a movie screen on the inside of your forehead. Practice seeing the outer picture on your inner mental screen. Don't try to force the experience. Again, look at the picture for a few minutes, then close your eyes and practice seeing the picture on your mental screen. Do this several times until you can see the picture with your eyes closed.

Now, visualize yourself in the picture, the way you would act if (or when) the picture becomes reality. The more you do this kind of exercise, the better you will be at doing it and therefore give power to the prayers you picture in your mind.

Visualization is one of the first spiritual tools I learned to use after discovering Unity School of Christianity. Many years ago, when I first started seriously reading Unity's publication, the *Daily Word*, I saw an advertisement for spiritual retreats. Immediately, I knew I wanted to go to the Unity campus located just outside of Kansas City, Missouri for the experience.

At the time, there appeared to be obstacles to me taking a week-long trip away from my young daughter and my job. At the time, the necessary finances were not in place for such a trip. But I got a picture of Unity Village, and in my prayer time each day, I saw myself approaching the facility. It was just a few months later that the funds I needed to go, the time off from my job, and the babysitter I needed for my young daughter all fell into place smoothly; I knew I was meant to go. This was just the first of many times I would be grateful to have access to spiritual tools that enhance my life.

The prayer anchor for this chapter tells us of a great remedy for moving forward in our lives, "Lift up your eyes." When we look away from the physical, or what's going on in our outer world, we can vision the possibility of better outcomes. Whenever we look away from or beyond "what is" we are uniquely positioned to attract "what can be." When we strongly feel the presence of our good and can imagine it to be so, we activate our God-given mental capacity to draw to us what our Creator has so lovingly assured us can be ours.

Prayer Practice

The idea here is to see yourself fully enjoying the good for which you are praying. See it in your mind's eye as you would like to experience it. Collect pictures of whatever you desire to manifest as a result of your specific prayer. These days, with the Internet and computer graphic enhancements, it is possible to access pictures of anything and everything you desire.

Visualize yourself in the pictures. Take the time to select pictures that are attractive and colorful—they will make more of an impression on your mind. When you look at your pictures, they should arouse your desire for what you are praying about. It is important that you see yourself in the pictures doing, being, and having the experience that you desire.

In your visualization, you may string a series of pictures together and form your own movie with other characters, music, etc. Be the star of the movie as well as the director. When you feel you have sufficiently experienced your desire within, to the point of feeling that it is real, then you have visualized your prayer. Close your time of prayerful visualization with a statement that is something like, *"I am grateful for this or whatever is for my greatest good and in accordance with God's divine plan for me."*

Use your pictures daily during your prayer time. With your eyes closed, practice seeing yourself experiencing the desire you are praying about. Speak aloud prayer statements that support your desires, such as *"I am _____*(fill in your prayer statement)" or *"I see myself _____*(fill in the blank)." Continue to use the pictures until you have your desire firmly envisioned in your mind. When you can close your eyes and see yourself with your desire, you may release the pictures and rely on your imagination. With a strong command of your imagination and the practice of seeing your desires, you'll achieve what you want or something even greater.

6

Pray for Your Loved Ones

Prayer Anchor: "I thank my God upon every remembrance of you, always in every prayer of mine making request for you all with joy."

Philippians 1:3-4 (NKJV)

Since no one exists in the world alone, it should be a routine practice for us to pray for those who are closest to us—family, friends, and those we consider our loved ones. Some people are so close to us and play such a valuable part in our life that their health, happiness, and well-being are intertwined with ours. To pray for them is only natural. Moreover, to pray for them on a regular basis is just wise and is an act of love.

There is a more personal side of why we pray for others. If we want a steady flow of good circulating in our lives, we should make it a habit of regularly and consistently praying for others. Each time we pray for someone else, we are blessed in the process.

Throughout the scriptures, we see friends, families, and members of spiritual communities praying with and for each other. Most religious and spiritual movements teach and practice some method of praying for others. Through various teachings, we're exposed to the importance of praying for others, starting with those closest to us.

In the garden of Gethsemane, Jesus asks those closest to him, his disciples, to pray with him. This lets us know that no matter who we are, we appreciate the prayers of others and especially from those who are most familiar with us.

However, there is an important lesson to remember regarding praying for loved ones. I remember many years ago a young woman asked me to pray with her that her boyfriend's wife would divorce him so that he could marry her. While she assured me that it was his desire to leave his wife for her, I noticed that she showed up alone to make her prayer request. While I could not pray as she wanted me to, I did say a prayer with her for divine order. We joined together in affirming that God's will be manifest for all concerned in the situation. She left unhappy with the prayer. I could not and would not presuppose to know the inner desires of all those involved or what would represent their highest good, and I did not choose to know.

Whenever we pray for others, we must surrender our personal will and trust that a larger plan exists for their lives than what we are privy to. I once had a woman come to me to pray with her that her son would find a nice girl, settle down, and get married because that's what she wanted for him. I prayed a prayer of divine order with her, affirming that God's divine plan would unfold for her son. Some years later, I spoke with her and learned that since our prayer together, her son had confided in her that he was gay and had been afraid to tell her. When we pray for others, their true desires may be beyond our human awareness, personal understanding, and knowledge. Our prayers can be most effective for our loved ones when we trust that God knows the intricate details of their circumstances and the outcomes that will support their highest good.

While there may be times when we feel compelled to use the power of prayer to infuse our own desires into the lives of our loved ones, let us avoid praying for specific outcomes without their permission. The most effective prayer I believe we can say and a safe alternative to specific prayers for others is: "God's will be done."

Prayer Practice

Find a prayer that you particularly like and pray it for your loved ones every day. Some suggestions are the Lord's Prayer or Psalm 23. There are also many books of prayer from which you can select prayers that are right for you and your loved ones, or you may compose a prayer of your own.

Prayers of protection, guidance, and peace are part of my personal prayer practice for my loved ones. Every day, I pray the same prayer for them. I may change a word here and there from time to time, but overall I want God's light, love, and presence to surround and enfold them wherever they are. Regardless of what is going on in their affairs, my prayer is consistent and a sincere desire for God's will, not mine, to be done in their lives. If they ask me to pray for specific situations, then I will include their requests in my prayer.

Consistency is important. Focusing daily attention on the well-being of your loved ones will be more helpful than a sporadic reaction to life's challenges. Make your prayer for your loved ones a daily habit and an important part of your personal prayer practices.

In his teachings, Jesus models a three-step process of first praying for himself, second praying for those closest to him, and third praying for all others. Do not underestimate the good you can do by taking time daily to hold your loved ones in prayer. We may not be able to physically do anything to help those we love through life's challenges, but we can always say a powerful prayer on their behalf—and that may be the spark to ignite a blessing into manifestation.

7

Prayer Partners

<u>Prayer Anchor</u>: 'For where two or three are gathered together in My name, I am there in the midst of them."

Matthew 18:20 (NKJV)

Nothing will enhance your prayers more than having a prayer partner, or a group of prayer partners who believe in the power of joint prayer. When you have the support of those who regularly join you in faith-centered, uplifting, affirmative prayer, you will magnify your potential to realize answered prayers.

In Jesus' teachings, we find spiritual principles by which to live, but Jesus also modeled his teachings with his actions. On several occasions, Jesus met with his prayer partners for support. In the seventeenth chapter of the gospel according to Matthew, Jesus led Peter, James, and John up a high mountain. The mountain represents a prayerful state of consciousness, where they went to be alone and pray together.

In this particular instance, the scripture describes the result of that powerful prayer experience: "And he was transfigured before them, and his face shone like the sun, and his clothes became dazzling white."[1] Pretty powerful results! Jesus had a vision from God, and it was so powerful that it changed Jesus from within and was reflected in his outer appearance in the presence of his prayer partners. We know that prayer does not change God; it changes us. We want to be changed so that we may be channels for the goodness of God to manifest.

This brings us to the value of having two or more positive-minded people who believe in us and in the power of prayer. Our best prayer partners will be those who can see us from a spiritual perspective and with faith in our ability to overcome challenges and thrive toward our goals. Solid prayer partner relationships give our prayers greater power if we have aligned ourselves with those who can see in us the potential that we may not see in ourselves.

Having a prayer partner or partners in no way diminishes or demeans the power we gain in silent communion alone with God. It is another method we may use to expand our prayer consciousness. Certainly, Jesus prayed alone as a testimony to the importance of our one-on-one time with God. Yet there were times when he wanted the prayer support of others.

There may also be times when your prayer partners can only give you their presence; they can be available and accessible to you, and that may be all they can give at the moment, but it may also be just what you need at the time. Never under estimate the appreciation of the touch of the hand, an embrace or a smile—at times, these can be as comforting as prayerful words spoken aloud.

Sometimes folks are reluctant to ask for prayer. Sometimes we'd rather suffer silently than let someone else know that we need help because we think it is a sign of weakness. Yet if we want to demonstrate our inner strength, we must ask for help when we need it and when we want it. In so doing, we find an inner courage that empowers us to find the solutions and answers we desire. Jesus tells us, and models for us, that prayer partnering is a tool we may use. Praying with and for others is another way we can harness greater spiritual power for ourselves.

Prayer Practice

Select your prayer partners (or partner) carefully. You want to pray with those who are like minded, who have similar religious or spiritual beliefs and values. Your prayer partners will be those who will support and encourage you to advance toward your desires without criticism or judgment. This is one of the benefits in being a member of a spiritual community. You will be drawn to certain people within that community, and certain people will be drawn to you. Your chances of finding someone who is suited to you as a prayer partner (or member of your prayer group) is enhanced within your spiritual network.

When you find someone who you feel may be a possible candidate as a prayer partner, discuss the idea with that person. If you are putting together a prayer group, discuss the opportunity with the candidates to determine if it is a harmonious match. Have a discussion about confidentiality concerning what is shared so that you each feel comfortable expressing your true concerns in prayer. Establish that the purpose is for prayer support, not for giving advice or counseling. Let your desires be made known, and ask your partner(s) how he or she would like to be supported if you were to pursue such a relationship. You and your candidates might even pray together about the decision to become prayer partners before establishing a relationship.

Suggest a time period for the relationship, such as two months. This will allow all partners to determine if a longer commitment is workable.

Sometimes a prayer partner relationship is a natural fit. In fact, certain relationships lend themselves for partnering in prayer— between spouses, family members, best friends, and even business associates. As part of the commitment to serve on the board of trustees at my church, board members serve as prayer partners to each other throughout their term in office. Each board member made the commitment to pray together from a structured prayer format once each week. I can say it has made for good relationships among the members throughout their terms—and proved to be a blessing to the ministry.

Look among the people in your life to see what relationships lend themselves to mutual support through prayer. Seek out those with a similar consciousness, goals, interests, and desires. Once you've found a partner, set a regular time when you are going to meet in person or contact each other by phone for your time of prayer. It is best to set a definite time frame within which the prayer is to take place. If there is no set time limit, social conversation may go on and on until the praying becomes less and less. Consider a prayer time of once a week for about fifteen to thirty minutes—depending on your format and the number of partners.

Agree on a format that will work for you and your prayer partners. You may use an inspirational reading, scripture, or affirmation. I strongly recommend a structured approach, especially for those who are new to praying in a group. Once the format is set, the group may decide to make changes to the process that will strengthen the unity and effectiveness of the group. Enjoy the added benefit of the close relationships that often form as a result of the powerful connection gained by shared faith, great expectation, and awesome results.

Part 2

Prayer Practices for Special Blessings

8

Bless Your House

Prayer Anchor: "And He said to them, 'It is written, 'My house shall be called a house of prayer,'..."

Matthew 21:13 (NKJV)

When I was a little girl, I used to sing a song with the words "Bless this house, O Lord we pray, make it safe by night and day." Even then, I believed in the benefits of blessing the house where one lives. The space where we eat our meals, enjoy our family and friends, sleep at night, and renew our minds is a sacred and holy space and deserves to be treated as such.

There are many good books written on space clearing and spiritual cleansing, so I will not try to imitate what others have done well. If you are not already in the habit of regularly clearing and cleansing your home, I recommend that you seek out some of these books and begin putting into practice the principle of clearing, cleansing, blessing, and praying up your house.

Also when I was a little girl, my mother had my siblings and I do some spring cleaning. We would discard old stuff we were no longer using or things that no longer worked. My mother would open all the windows and doors in the house on a Saturday in early springtime, and all of us kids would be put to work. With the smelly cleaning products my mother insisted we use, like ammonia, bleach, and vinegar, we would wash windows and walls, scrub floors, and clean the crystal chandelier in the dining room. We would also wash the bedding and towels, and hang them on the clothesline outside to dry. Then we would clean the kitchen. All the pots and pans would be taken out of the cabinets, and the inside of the cabinets were cleaned out so that we could rearrange the contents.

I remember thinking as a child, *When I grow up, I'm not going to make my children do all this hard work*. Guess what? I did, and yes, they complained.

But what I do remember enjoying is the fresh, clean smell and feel the house had after all the work was done. The house had a light and airy feel to it. It seemed like the way you'd want the house to be all the time. Perhaps you can relate to this.

Even today, I enjoy my home when it is orderly, clutter free, clean, smells of fragrances that uplift the spirit, and my belongings are arranged in a way that is aesthetically pleasing. I enjoy being in my home and feel better no matter how my day at the office has gone. Home feels safe, healthy, and uplifting.

In this chapter, I want to stress the importance of keeping your home free from clutter, keeping it clean, clearing the energy within it, and praying it up. I have performed a house blessing on several occasions when people first moved into a new home. However, I believe the best person to bless your house is you. This way, you infuse your own intention and energy into your environment.

Also a house blessing is not a one-time thing. I believe a house blessing should be done annually and, in certain instances, a few times a year. Other instances may be after some event of a challenging nature occurs in the home and when the home is in harm's way, like when a hurricane, tornado, or storm is headed your way.

There are certain circumstances when you may want a professional in space clearing to do this kind of work for you. Examples are when the energy is heavy or negative after a traumatic situation has occurred in the home (for example, when life is tragically taken in the house, after a home invasion, a difficult divorce, or you are made aware that the previous inhabitants were living a negative lifestyle).

There are people who do this kind of work, such as spiritual or feng shui practitioners. Get suggestions from those in your spiritual community, or some New Age stores may be able to recommend a person who is skilled at this work. However, anyone you know with a strong prayer consciousness will be a good candidate to assist you. Use wisdom when selecting the person and pray to be guided to them.

You may choose to have a consecrated space in your home where you perform your daily prayers. This may include setting up an altar or several altars in your home to help facilitate your prayer efforts. Once your space is cleared of clutter and negative energy, pray up the space. Make your house a house of prayer by praying in it, for it, and all through it.

The main thing to remember is to keep your house in order and filled with positive energy. Learn some of the cleansing ceremonies and rituals for clearing space; they may become a part of your regular spiritual practices.

Prayer Practice

I recommend including a scripture as part of your house blessing. I use the Lord's Prayer and Psalms 23 and 91. You may use other blessings along with these, but I like beginning my blessing with scripture to give my house blessing my own favored spiritual foundation.

This is the basic house blessing I use, and suggest you give your home this type of treatment once or twice a year. Be sure to do a blessing when you occupy your home for the first time. You may also choose to do a blessing after something has happened to cause you to believe there may be some blocked or negative energy in your home. Once you have done this level of blessing, you will probably just do a maintenance blessing once or twice a year.

- Use incense to clear the energy throughout the entire house. Set a mental intention that you are clearing away any negative or stale energy in your home. Walk the inner perimeter of the house slowly, gently waving a stick of incense. (I suggest using frankincense and myrrh, sage, or sandalwood.) Then, light incense in each and every room and let it burn to completion.

- Light a white candle in each room. If possible, place the candle in the center of the room.

- From outside your home, face the main entrance and pray Psalm 23. Proceed inside, facing the main entrance headed outside, and again pray Psalm 23. Now from inside, pray Psalm 23 facing each entrance door of your house until every entrance and exit has been blessed with this Psalm.

- Next, starting from the inside of your front door, pray Psalm 91 as you walk from room to room.

- Pray the Lord's Prayer aloud in its entirety in every room of your house.

- Now begin speaking words of protection, health, and well-being in each room regarding the purpose of the space. Make up your own prayer for each room. Just speak from your heart the highest intentions you have for those who will occupy the space. Affirm that God's grace is always present and active in the space.

- Bless the kitchen for healthy, nourishing meals to be prepared there with love.

- Bless the bathrooms for divine elimination. (Yes, do this; it is important for good health.)

- Bless the family room for good, quality family time together in harmony, peace, and fun.

- Bless all bedrooms for all those who live in the house; use their names when you bless the rooms where they sleep. For example, when my son was a young boy, I would bless his room, when we first moved into a home and annually thereafter. I would say something like, "I am grateful that Benjamin is always divinely guided, guarded, and protected wherever he is and that this room is a restful, peaceful, happy place for him." (I should have added something about the cleanliness of it!) My son felt his room was his safe haven up until the time when he moved out and into his own space.

- Bless every room and space including laundry room, closets, garage, etc. Allow the candles you have placed to burn out completely.

- Place some fresh flowers in the main living areas of the house for the three days following the blessing. The beauty of flowers and their fragrance will be uplifting to the overall energy of your home.

- Immediately following your house blessing, be intentional about enjoying the peaceful, blessed energy you have created in your home. This is a great time to light a scented candle, have a special dinner for yourself and the family and add some relaxing music.

An exception to the annual or biannual house blessing is during times of preparation for severe weather conditions like hurricanes, tornadoes, and other storms. I recommend that you bless your home by praying Psalm 91 as you walk around the entire outside perimeter of your home. Then on the inside, from the center point of the home, affirm aloud the Lord's Prayer followed by Psalm 23. Finally, facing each of the four directions starting at the east, followed by south, west and north, pray Psalm 91.

As an ongoing spiritual practice, speak kind and loving words in every room of your house on a regular basis. Fill the air with healthy, peaceful energy, in this way you consecrate your house as one of prayer.

9

Bless Your Business

Prayer Anchor: "And He said to them, 'Why did you seek Me? Did you not know that I must be about My Father's business?'"

Luke 2:49 (NKJV)

Most of us, at one time or another, dream up some great invention, a clever product, or an idea that we would love to make available to the whole world. In the dream, our invention or product would succeed where others have failed. We would have the ideal product, the best people working for us, the perfect plan, and the money, fame, accolades, and fortune to prove it.

While dreams often manifest for us, we've also seen the dreams of mom-and-pop operations fold, and we've seen big businesses forced to file for bankruptcy. Every year, many businesses go belly up and are forced to close their doors. And we probably could not begin to imagine the many thousands of businesses that are just getting by or operating in the red.

I remember I went to a seminar many years ago about starting your own business. The seminar leader said up front, "Quite frankly, I want to talk you out of starting your own business. Most people have a romantic idea of what business ownership is, and the reality is that owning a business is tough work." When I left the seminar that day, I had the sense that entrepreneurship could be a great blessing or my worst nightmare.

Yet each year, many new businesses spring up with fresh enthusiasm for a chance at successful entrepreneurship. There is something fascinating about starting a new venture that we believe in. A special kind of energy propels the person who is inclined to pursue the manifestation of his or her idea into a living enterprise. I've felt it, and maybe you have to. Some of us even have what I call the "entrepreneur gene."

I first became aware of the entrepreneur gene by observing my mother. She had it. Her dream was to be a restaurant owner, and she became that several times. I worked in her restaurants as a young girl and had the opportunity to observe her passion, drive, and enthusiasm for her dream. She worked long hours and holidays, and it was never a chore for her. My mother loved to cook, and she did it with love. She was a good cook, her food was delicious, and her ideas were grand. Even up until the time she made her transition, she talked about ideas for the next restaurant she wanted to open.

While I do believe that we should all love what we do as our livelihood, those who possess the entrepreneur gene have the passion, drive and enthusiasm to relentlessly pursue their venture expecting it to thrive. Even still, we need something more if we want to be fulfilled by the work involved in being successful in our own business venture.

In the prayer anchor for this chapter, Jesus is a young boy, but he gives us sound advice that we can use for successfully owning and running a business of any kind. Jesus' parents had been searching for him, as he had been separated from them a few days prior. They found the boy in the temple doing what seemed to be natural to him and would later prove to be what he had passion, drive, and enthusiasm for.

His parents, obviously concerned for his well-being, on finding him asked him what he was doing. He said to them, "I must be about my Father's business." This is the successful ingredient that, when embraced, can assist in the fulfillment and success we desire in whatever business we're guided to embark on.

Jesus gets to the core of important issue. If we start a business, who will be head of it? Who will be its true owner? When we get the real issue regarding whose business we intend to operate, we're on our way to success.

Now let us acknowledge up front that every business that "appears" successful by the world's standard may not be founded on spiritual principles. In fact, we could say that many "successful endeavors" seem to be focused on money, power, and the desire for fame by the owner. This chapter speaks to those who desire to make a choice to believe a higher power is the source of great ideas and the resources that it will take to bring the idea into manifestation and allow it to be a blessing to others.

However, even if a business does appear to be successful *without* accessing spiritual principles, God's presence is still at work. From this viewpoint, God's presence is revealed in the goods and services supplied to customers, the blessings that manifest through the generosity of those who receive salaries, profits, dividends, as well as through the sharing of talents of those employed by the enterprise. This perspective allows me to believe God is the most influential and powerful business partner an entrepreneur could ever have—the possibilities for people to be blessed are far reaching.

If we acknowledge a business idea as being divinely inspired, we will have an attitude grounded in success. When we agree to take God's idea and be the hands and feet that will bring it into manifestation, we are not in business alone, but we have the most powerful and awesome business partner available to all humankind. God never fails, and neither shall we if we are, as Jesus said, "about our Father's business."

In 1 Chronicles, King David models what being about our Father's business looks like: "Therefore David blessed the LORD before all the assembly; and David said: "Blessed are You, LORD God of Israel, our Father, forever and ever. Yours, O LORD, is the greatness, The power and the glory, The victory and the majesty; For all *that is* in heaven and in earth *is Yours;* Yours *is* the kingdom, O LORD, And You are exalted as head over all."[1]

David takes no credit for all the gifts the people have brought to build the temple. He is doing the work of God on behalf of the divine idea given to him. David is the one who gets up early in the morning, stays up late at night, works holidays, makes the deals that need to be made, works with the staff, and does all that it takes to run the day-to-day operations. However, when it comes time to give accolades, David gives all honor and praise to God for what is being done. David acknowledges God's ownership and leadership over the building of the temple and gives God all the credit before the people.

"Both riches and honor *come* from You, And You reign over all. In Your hand *is* power and might; In Your hand *it is* to make great And to give strength to all."[2] David knows that the resources—money, people, talent, ideas—are in the hands of God. David knows he can be successful in this building project only if he recognizes, acknowledges, and leads with God as the true leader. While David is king and has assumed the role of leader, in his heart and mind, God, working in and through him, leads the way to his success.

"Now therefore, our God, We thank You And praise Your glorious name."[3] David takes the time to give thanks for the works that have been done, the resources, and the people who have participated in and blessed God's enterprise.

"O LORD our God, all this abundance that we have prepared to build You a house for Your holy name is from Your hand, and *is* all Your own."[4] The resources needed for building the lavish temple were not just provided, but there was an abundance. David again acknowledges God as the provider. What a great lesson for all who have the desire to start, own, and run a business from a spiritual perspective. I love this story because David is surely putting in many hours being king, using his talents to inspire and motivate his people, but by his own admission, God is the true business owner, and David makes it clear he works for God.

The moral of the story is this: if you want to be successful in any business, the riches and honor will come when you acknowledge it as God's business and operate it using divine guidance and wisdom.

But we cannot end this discussion without mentioning two additional points. With this great success story unfolding, there were offerings, celebrations, and the pouring of libations. "And they made sacrifices to the LORD and offered burnt offerings to the LORD on the next day: a thousand bulls, a thousand rams, a thousand lambs, with their drink offerings, and sacrifices in abundance for all Israel."[5] Offerings were made as an outer symbol of thanks to God. In today's terms, we would tithe to the place where we get our spiritual nourishment. (And, yes, businesses should tithe from the net profits or have a commitment to consistently give back to the community through charitable donations.)

The celebration was grand and lavish; it was an outer reward for the people who worked diligently toward the success of the business. In today's terms, employees, vendors, and volunteers would be acknowledged and appreciated for their efforts.

The pouring of libation was a drink offering, most likely of wine. It was made as a sacrifice to God, acknowledging blessings received. In Western culture, we don't generally find the pouring of libation, we could however have someone that we honor and hold in high esteem give a toast at a celebration or banquet. Gratitude and thanksgiving would be the sentiment behind the toast. We lift our glasses, speak a heartfelt thank you, and affirm continued health, success, prosperity, and well-being, all to the glory of God.

David was a great example of a divinely guided leader. When guided to pass the leadership role to his son, he did everything to prepare Solomon for the position. David prepared Solomon by being an example of a God-centered leader. When the time came, Solomon was anointed, meaning a special blessing was conferred on him, and everyone respected the son because the father had prepared him well. "And give my son Solomon a loyal heart to keep Your commandments and Your testimonies and Your statutes, to do all *these things,* and to build the temple for which I have made provision. So they ate and drank before the LORD with great gladness on that day. And they made Solomon the son of David king the second time, and anointed *him* before the LORD *to be* the leader, and Zadok *to be* priest. Then Solomon sat on the throne of the LORD as king instead of David his father, and prospered; and all Israel obeyed him. All the leaders and the mighty men, and also all the sons of King David, submitted themselves to King Solomon. So the LORD exalted Solomon exceedingly in the sight of all Israel, and bestowed on him *such* royal majesty as had not been on any king before him in Israel."[6]

Any good business idea deserves a succession plan that will allow it to live out its full life span, even if that takes it beyond our leadership tenure. If the endeavor is a God-inspired idea, we know it is not ours to possess or covet. We want to see it go forward even when it is time for us to retire or move on to another venture. If we truly care about the idea, the source of the idea, and those who can be blessed by the idea, we can make the choice to run and operate the business with this philosophy from day one. We build in our thoughts early on methods to pass on the blessings of the business beyond our involvement.

How may we be in business and operate it from a position that allows us to claim that "we are about our Father's business"? We keep in mind that God is the source of divine ideas and that if we allow it, we shall be supplied with the guidance and resources we need to succeed; the beauty of this business model is that God never fails.

Prayer Practice

Pray about the idea you have for a business until you feel it is indeed a divine idea. Often when ideas come, they need refining through prayer. Ask for guidance and wisdom as you gather your facts and figures and make the necessary inquiries. Use the prayer practices in this book to ground your decision in faith, love, and wisdom.

Oftentimes, when people have asked me to bless their business, they are talking about the physical space where the business will be located. But as the business owner, you should receive the first blessing. You can do the blessing yourself or have your prayer partners or a prayer group that supports you do a special blessing for you.

In that blessing, you want to be anointed. Speak words with power to the effect that you are empowered with wisdom and spiritual courage to follow God's guidance, that you are compassionate in all your interactions with others, and that you always remember God as your source.

Pray verses of scripture that ground you in spiritual awareness, such as "Let the words of my mouth and the meditation of my heart Be acceptable in Your sight, O LORD, my strength and my Redeemer";[7] or "Teach me good judgment and knowledge, For I believe Your commandments."[8]

Sit with the name of the business in your time of meditation. You want a name that is unique and divine for your particular business purpose. Affirm that God is the source of the idea for the business called _____and that God is the source of its prosperity.

When your physical business location is selected (which should be done prayerfully, of course), the space itself needs to be blessed.

- Before you occupy the space, do a space clearing with incense over a three-day period. For each of the three days, walk through the space while gently waving an incense stick (for example, frankincense and myrrh, sage, or sandalwood) with the intention of ridding the space of any negative energy. As you walk through the space, say Psalm 23 at least three times. Burn incense in each room for three days.

- During the same three-day period, burn candles in all the rooms. The business owner will have three candles lit in his or her space: a white candle representing the spiritual presence of God, a yellow candle representing divine wisdom, and a purple candle for wealth and spiritual power. With the lighting of each candle, affirm *"Let there be light."*

- Near the front door, burn a green candle for growth and prosperity. A sample scripture to affirm when you light the candle is *"Deal bountifully with Your servant, that I may live and keep Your word."*[9]

- If there will be employees, burn candles in the space they will occupy according to the intention you want to set for their particular positions. Use yellow for creativity, orange for hospitality, and green for finance or simply use white.

- On the fourth day, place a healthy green plant at the door of your individual work area or at the front entrance of the business. A healthy green plant symbolizes growth— and that is what you want for your business.

Now the space is ready to occupy. Again set your intention with every decoration and every piece of furniture you place. Have in mind that you are setting up an environment to support health, wealth, success, and happiness in all that you do on behalf of the business.

Finally you are ready to have a celebration with friends and supporters who will bring their positive energy to you, the business, and the space. This is your public blessing for you and the business. Shape the blessing after King David's example in the form of prayer and ceremony.

- Acknowledge God as the owner and true leader of the enterprise.

- Affirm the idea as a divine one for which God will provide the necessary resources in abundance.

- Know that as God's living enterprise, you have full access to the inexhaustible supply of riches and honor.

- Commit yourself to be open and receptive to God's guidance in all that you do on behalf of the divine idea that has been given you.

- Set the intention to regularly acknowledge God for the success of the business as it grows and prospers.

- Plan to make regular tithes and/or charitable offerings and do so with the same enthusiasm with which you receive the riches and honor that are sure to come in abundance.

Have someone give a powerful toast (use sparkling cider if you will not use champagne or wine). With God as your partner and well-meaning friends, food, and music added to the celebration, your business will be blessed for success—the rest will be up to you.

10

Bless Your Pet

Prayer Anchor: "Then God blessed them, and God said to them, 'Be fruitful and multiply; fill the earth and subdue it; have dominion over the fish of the sea, over the birds of the air, and over every living thing that moves on the earth.'"

Genesis 1:28 (NKJV)

From the beginning, animals have been part of our lives. Our prayer anchor reveals that humankind has a responsibility to care for animals. After all, God blessed every living thing that moves, and we should be accountable for the role of dominion we have been entrusted with.

Many of us have pets, but they are more than that—they are part of our family. We love them, care for them, and feed them, and they demonstrate love for us, so certainly they deserve to be blessed just like any other member of the family.

Animals provide special lessons that we may learn from when we are open to them. Those who have pets cherish their loving presence. It is always amazing to watch the animals and discover the personality and energy they bring to the household.

Many studies have shown that the love and companionship of a dog or cat can boost someone's mental state. Pets seem to have the gift that we humans are working on: unconditional love. Dogs have been called man's best friend for this reason. Imagine how easy it would be to experience unconditional love without the capacity to judge others. So it is with our pets: they love us with no judgment or criticism, only the desire to be there for us and with us.

I always recommend that people who live alone have some other "life-giving" energy in their home. If no animal particularly suits you, consider an aquarium with a few fish or simply place a couple of houseplants to provide uplifting, life-giving energy. Life-giving energy can elevate the mood in the space and help keep us in tune with growth while stimulating our thoughts of well-being.

A pet is a great idea if you are willing to take on the responsibility of caring for one. And yes, pets do require and deserve to be well cared for. Caring for a pet has many similarities to caring for a child, so make the decision to own a pet carefully.

In the book of Genesis, we are told that humankind has dominion over animals. I believe that dominion means we are responsible for their well-being. Dominion gives us the task of stewardship to provide for their needs physically and emotionally. As one creation of God to another, we must do whatever we can to assure that their journey in life is healthy and happy, and what a joy it can be.

Prayer Practice

If you bring a pet into your home, make it part of the family. Your pet should have his or her own space like every member of the household. When you bless the rest of the house, make sure that you bless the space where your pet relaxes and sleeps. Include your pet when you bless the other members of the family. Bless the meals that you serve your pet.

Those who are not pet owners and lovers may say that you are going overboard, but you have accepted the charge of stewardship seriously. You enjoy the love shared between you and your pet, and that is what counts.

Here is a blessing you can say for your pet: *"Thank you, God, for the gift of _____(pet's name). I behold him (or her) as your special creation. I celebrate his (or her) presence in my life and my presence in his (or her) life. I bless the closeness we share and this opportunity to participate in loving kindness. Thank you, God, for _____."*

Say aloud to your beloved pet often," _____(pet's name), you are God's special creation. God's love surrounds you in safety, protection, health, and well-being wherever you are, now and always. You are God's blessed gift to me, and I am grateful for your presence in my life."

11

Safe Travels

<u>Prayer Anchor:</u> "So Jacob went on his
way, and the angels of God met him."

Genesis 32:1 (NKJV)

Traveling nowadays can be frustrating, demanding, and challenging.
But I can think back to a time when traveling was a bit gentler on
the mind and body. I remember the times when I would arrive at
the airport just one hour before the flight, check my bag with ease,
board the plane in an expedient and orderly fashion, be served
a full meal with a beverage (in coach class), enjoy a movie, land
safely, pick up my bag without delay, and be out of the airport and
on my way. Oh, "the good old days."

I also remember when I could fill up the gas tank in my 1973
Chevrolet Monte Carlo for just $5. I drove that beautiful gold and
black car everywhere. It was nothing to drive out of town for an
enjoyable weekend and return home with change in my pocket and
the gas tank still a quarter full.

Even before my flying days and before owning my car, I once
traveled with my mom to Providence, Rhode Island, by train from
Detroit, Michigan. It was great. Mom and I boarded easily, sat in
comfortable seats, ate in the dining car, and enjoyed the beautiful
scenery between stops. The journey was long, but eventually we
arrived at our destination safely.

Today, whenever I travel, I bless the journey before me. Whenever my children and loved ones travel, I bless the journey they take. When I fly, I bless the airplane, the pilots, and everyone on board. Whenever I drive, I bless my car. It is comforting for me to bless my travels. It often keeps me from being frustrated when I'm waiting in a long line at the airport or when I, despite perfect directions, end up driving on the wrong highway forty miles out of the way.

In 2005, after Hurricane Wilma, for those of us in Miami who were left in the path of Wilma's destruction, we had difficulty getting gasoline. Gas lines were long and some folks waited for hours. It was definitely a time when a travel blessing was needed. Would it have made the lines move any faster? I don't know, but I do know that anxiety levels were high, tempers were short, and patience was significantly low. Peace, harmony, and a spirit of cooperation would have helped the stress that many folks expressed in various ways.

When we travel, we want to be like Jacob. We want the angels of God to meet us on our journey—whether those angels show up in physical form, divine ideas, or intuitive messages from within. We want our travels to be blessed with the assurance that we will arrive at our destination safely with few disruptions. We want to be met with experiences that enhance the fun and joy of going new places, meeting new people, or seeing old friends. We desire God's angels to help with the details of our journey so that we may experience the difference between a good trip and a great trip. We would like to know that we have God's blessings on all the journeys we make. That's why a travel blessing can help. The details of the trip may or may not be challenging, but you will have assurance that through it all God's presence goes with you.

When I think of traveling, I think of the movie *Planes, Trains, and Automobiles* starring John Candy and Steve Martin. What started out as a normal business trip turned into a traveler's nightmare. Nothing seemed to go their way, no matter how they traveled—by plane, train, or automobile. By the end of the movie, what appeared to be a chance meeting between these two men, joined together by a series of travel disasters, turned out to be the beginning of a new friendship.

Even if we make all the preparations and say all the blessings we know, what appears to be the worst trip in terms of travel mishaps can still turn out to be an unexpected gift. Your trip will be so much more enjoyable with the conscious intention to remain calm through any delays, miscommunications, and detours. If you can be at peace within, the outer journey will follow your lead. And who knows what angels you'll meet in the process or what wonderful gifts await you on the journey to your destination?

When you bless your travels in advance, you are praying up the entire experience. You set an intention that your trip will be blessed and that angels of God will meet you on your way. However, I have discovered that much of my own travel success occurs when I have done my part in preparing for the journey. Little things like taking my car for a checkup before driving on a long trip, keeping my valuables with me when I travel by plane, or making sure my passport is in order well in advance of my international voyages can make a big difference in my experience.

Blessing your trip with a prayer is no substitute for doing your part in planning and preparation. For your travels, plan carefully, bless your journey with prayer, set your intention for a safe and successful trip, and then go, expecting to meet angels of God along the way.

Prayer Practice

Take time to plan your trip in detail, from what to pack, checking the weather forecast, having adequate directions, making sure you have proper identification, securing your credit cards, etc. Do not underestimate your ability to make your travels successful by doing your part with the details.

Once you've done your part with the preparation, it is time to bless your journey.

- Before you leave, bless your home with a brief prayer. Say your own prayer, but here is a simple example: *"I am grateful that this house is divinely protected in my absence. The peaceful presence and power of God watches over this home day and night."* You may not think this is so important, but during one of the many hurricane warnings that occurred one year in Miami, I blessed my home and left before the storm hit. As I was driving back to the area four days later, I did not know what shape my home would be in. The reports were that a lot of damage had been done, with few people having electricity. When I arrived, my home had a few tiles missing from my roof, and my fence, which had already been in disrepair, was down. Several of my neighbors had a lot more damage than I did, but my neighborhood was one of the few that had electricity. From the appearance of the items in my refrigerator, I had lost electricity for only a short time. There were neighborhoods in Miami that did not have electricity for a month. Bless your home before you leave it to set in your mind that it is divinely protected.

- Say a prayer of blessing for yourself before you leave your home, saying something like *"God's presence goes before me, making my journey safe, smooth, and successful in every way. I travel under the grace of God, and only good can meet me on this journey."* If others are traveling with you, have them join you in the prayer. If you are traveling by automobile remember to bless it also.

- If you are traveling by plane or train, it is important to bless the vehicle once you are on it. Say something like *"God's loving presence surrounds this _____ (airplane, train, bus, etc.) and every person on it. God is directing the _____ (pilot, conductor, bus driver, etc.) with divine wisdom and good choices. We travel with ease and under grace, arriving safely at our destination."*

- When you are ready to return home from your trip, say another blessing for yourself and anyone who is traveling with you. Of course, bless the mode of transportation that brings you safely back home just as you did before you left.

- When you arrive home, give thanks that all is well. For example, *"I am grateful to know that all is well with my home. The peaceful presence and power of God continues to watch over this home day and night. I (we) live in this home that is always blessed by the grace of God."*

As you travel, depend on God's presence no matter the circumstances of your journey. Take every opportunity to bless your travels with a prayer of guidance, wisdom, protection, safety and joy. Have the idea firmly fixed in your mind that wherever you go, you are always divinely enfolded in God's care and keeping.

12

Claim Overflowing Blessings

Prayer Anchor: "Bring the full tithe into the storehouse, so that there may be food in my house, and thus put me to the test, says the Lord of hosts; see if I will not open the windows of heaven for you and pour down for you an overflowing blessing."

Malachi 3:10 (NRSV)

What does tithing have to do with prayer? Everything. Just as prayer is an act of faith, so is tithing. When we pray, we acknowledge God as the source from which we expect our answers to come. When we tithe, we acknowledge that God is the source of what we have already received as well as the inexhaustible supply from which more is to come.

Tithing is a prayer in and of itself. It is a prayer of gratitude, celebration, and joyful expectation for continued blessings. When we give ten percent of our income to a place that represents God, usually a religious or spiritual organization, we are acknowledging the gifts God has already provided for us. At the same time, we are making a spiritual investment toward future blessings that are sure to follow.

When we were children, our parents taught us that when someone gives us something, we should say thank you. When we tithe, it is a form of expressing a sincere thank you to God for what we have received. The expression of our gratitude aligns us with a consciousness to attract even more.

The prayer anchor for this chapter tells us to try tithing. The promise is that we will be rewarded with overflowing blessings for our faithful actions. Before I put God to the test—this test of tithing, that is—I used to think that tithing was something preachers made up to coerce people into giving money to the church. I didn't have much money in those days and didn't see any purpose in giving it to the church. I felt like I needed my money more that the church did. I figured the preacher made a higher salary than me and so did the other people sitting in the pews. In my mind, it stood to reason that when the preacher started talking about tithing, he was talking to the other folks in church, not to me.

It was not until I found myself in the place where my life was in such dire shape that I was finally willing to at least listen to the tithing message. My health, relationships, and finances were all failing, and I was desperate to consider solutions to my challenges that I was not previously open to—yes, even tithing.

I decided to take the scripture from Malachi to heart. I read it over and over again to make sure I understood it. The more I read, the more interested I became in seeing just what God could do in my life if I tithed. Skeptically, after weeks of putting myself through an inner struggle, I chose to try it because I wanted the "windows of heaven to pour down for me an overflowing blessing."

The next Sunday, I signed up to volunteer with the youth education ministry as a way of tithing my talents. On the same Sunday, when the offering basket came around, I held onto my envelope tightly; it was as if I was about to give up everything I owned at that moment. Inside the envelope was ten percent of the income I had received that week. It was a leap of faith to release the envelope, particularly when I was working hard to barely cover my living expenses.

Holding my tithe, I recited the offering blessing along with the other givers. By this time, I had memorized Malachi 3:10, so, still holding the envelope tightly, I recited it to myself. I needed the assurance that I could expect my "overflowing blessing." I finally placed the envelope into the offering basket.

I continued to recite the scripture as I gave my financial tithe each week and volunteered with the youth education ministry. The prayer seemed to work. Tithing seemed to work. Things got better in my life for a while, but once things got better, I stopped reading and reciting Malachi 3:10 and stopped tithing. Somehow I erroneously thought that I had received my overflowing blessings, and I would keep receiving them even after I had stopped giving. Over time, things got increasingly worse. Before long, my affairs seemed to be worse than they were before.

It took several years of tithing off and on until I made a conscious, whole-hearted commitment to regular prayer, volunteering my talents, and tithing. Like many folks, I love to receive, but giving had somehow eluded my understanding as being an affirmation of gratitude for answered prayer and the many blessings in my life. I had not connected tithing with my faith in God and the promises revealed to the prophet Malachi thousands of years ago. I had no problem asking God for what I needed, but I didn't think that giving had much to do with my receiving. It took years, but I did eventually get Jesus' message: "give, and it will be given to you. A good measure, pressed down, shaken together, running over, will be put into your lap; for the measure you give will be the measure you get back."[1]

I have been committed to tithing for many years. Today, I enjoy giving as a demonstration of my faith and gratitude for all that I can be, have, and do. I have included tithing in *Pray Up Your Life* because giving is an important part of spiritual growth.

Years ago, I misunderstood the purpose of tithing by focusing on the preacher and other congregants, so I present tithing here so you don't misunderstand this spiritual practice. In no way am I attempting to coerce anyone into giving to a particular church, denomination, or spiritual teacher, but rather I present giving as a consciousness to be attained for greater spiritual development.

I will be the first to tell you that if you are not willing to learn the lessons inherent in generous, anxiety-free giving, then tithing is a bitter pill to swallow. So let us look at the tools that will help you understand the basics of tithing and support you in becoming a consistent, cheerful giver.

What is a tithe?

We first see tithing mentioned in the Bible in Genesis 14, where Abram gives a tenth of all that he collected from the spoils of a battle to King Melchizedek who was "priest of God Most High."[2]

Ten percent of all the income you receive is given with love and gratitude to the place where you get your spiritual nourishment. (Hopefully, you are receiving spiritual nourishment from somewhere.)

We tithe our time and spiritual gifts as well. When we give our attention to studying, learning, reading, praying, and meditating, we are giving back to God from the time we have been given. Tithing of our spiritual gifts or talents means we find a place to be of service. Whatever skills we have to give in service, we express our gratitude by helping others with the abilities God has given us.

Where should you give your tithe?

In tithing to a church or a spiritual center, you must ask yourself, "Do I believe and trust that this organization represents God, God's work, and purpose for the lives of the people who attend, the people it serves, and the greater community?"

Whether you tithe your time, spiritual gifts, talents, or money, you should feel that the place where you give your tithe represents high spiritual ideals through its members' works and teachings. If you tithe to an individual, your questions should be the same. The place where you tithe should be the place where you are continually reminded and involved in God's love, peace, truth, and prosperity.

For a business, tithing is more along the lines of charitable giving and would be provided from its net profit. This type of giving will be to the community or worthy causes that help fulfill the mission and vision of the company. Many businesses donate to non-profit organizations and offer sponsorships to worthy community events—if this equals ten percent of net profits, this could be viewed as a tithe.

Why tithe?

The bigger, more important question is, do you want the "windows of heaven to pour upon you overflowing blessings"? Giving and receiving represents two sides of the same spiritual law. If we receive, we must complete the transaction by giving. As we give, we set a cycle of activity in motion—that of giving and receiving. The more we give, the more we can expect to receive, and a continuous flow of giving and receiving keeps our good circulating.

When should you tithe?

As soon as you have something with which to tithe—time, spiritual gifts, talents, and/or money—that's when you tithe. When you wake up in the morning and realize you have been blessed with another day, spend time in prayer, meditation, or in a spiritual devotional activity. Be open to opportunities to be of service in your neighborhood or spiritual community.

If you receive your income weekly, tithe weekly; if money comes to you monthly, tithe monthly. If you receive an unexpected monetary gift (and if you are a tither, this will happen), write your tithe then or set the money apart to give it at the next opportunity. Some folks mail tithes to their church as soon as they write the check to keep their good circulating. With banking capabilities today, we can make a tithe electronically as soon as we receive a blessing. The sooner we put giving into motion, do we activate an opportunity to receive.

Tithing is a practice that expands the generosity of your spirit. When you are a generous person, you draw the generosity of others toward you. You receive according to the level of generosity that you mirror in your experiences of giving.

Prayer Practice

If you are already a tither, then you know the value of giving to God's work. Longtime tithers discover that tithing trains us to be good spiritual givers in all areas of life. That is, giving becomes not so much our tithe but a way of life.

Most of the tithers I know give well above ten percent of their income and are active in serving others. Tithers are usually dedicated to their prayer life and the study of truth; it's what keeps them actively living the principle of giving and receiving.

Keep yourself grounded in faith in God and continue to express your gratitude in as many ways as you can. I suggest that you take time to read Malachi 3 and 4. Make a study of the deeper meaning of these chapters and how you may benefit from the teachings.

If you are not a tither, you may need some mental and emotional conditioning before you start to tithe financially. Read the prayer anchor for this chapter three times a day for twenty-one days. But don't just read the scripture; attempt to understand the message being conveyed through Malachi's revelation from God. During the twenty-one-day period, pray to have your consciousness of generosity opened to a new level so that you may regularly give with no thought of return and from a consciousness of faith and thanksgiving.

If you are grateful for what God has and is doing in your life, then let your giving reflect it. I never suggest that people begin attempting to tithe with anything less than ten percent. Why? The word "tithe" means a tenth. There is no such thing as a partial tithe. Tithing is an act of faith. If we do not put God to the full test, we are not putting our faith in God, and we are putting our trust in our circumstances. So if you're not ready to tithe, just keep giving at your current level as you read Malachi 3:10; when you have reached a level of faith where you are willing to take God's challenge, wholeheartedly give your tithe and do so consistently. There are many books on tithing and stewardship programs in many spiritual centers to help you embrace tithing with joy.

Find a place to volunteer your spiritual gifts or talents. If you are not ready to begin financial tithing, you can always start here and add financial tithing when you are ready. But plan on giving "the full tithe" of prayer time, spiritual gifts, talents, and finances. It all works together and constitutes full giving of the tithe.

Make it a practice to pray daily. That is the theme of this book. No matter what prayer you affirm or what scripture you read, the more time you spend with your mind and heart centered in God, the more you access your divine ability to live the quality of life that you deserve and desire. As you open your mind to a greater awareness of giving in all areas—time, service, and finances—your receiving consciousness will surely grow. Living from this new level of consciousness, you claim overflowing blessings for your life.

13

Pleasant Words, Healthy Body

<u>Prayer Anchor</u>: "Pleasant words are like a honeycomb,
Sweetness to the soul and health to the bones."

Proverbs 16:24 (NKJV)

As spiritual beings dressed in a physical body, we are responsible for maintaining the outfit we're wearing. But our Creator has truly blessed us by equipping us with many tools for this sometimes demanding task. When we use the spiritual and mental tools at our disposal, we can really take excellent care of the suit that covers our soul.

For example, we have the spiritual tools of prayer and meditation and the mental tools of life-affirming thoughts and words. There are also many tools we may use on the physical level. What a gift our Creator has given us that our minds and bodies have been so carefully and wisely designed that they respond with ease to the tools at our disposal. When we combine these tools to work toward the goal of self-care, we initiate the best health care plan a body could have, one that encompasses spirit, mind, and body.

Our successful personal health care plan can work like this: When we pray and meditate, we condition our thoughts. Thoughts shape ideas, and ideas come alive through our words. Words are like missionaries going out to fulfill the purpose for which they are spoken. "so shall my word be that goes forth from my mouth; it shall not return to me empty, but it shall accomplish that which I purpose, and succeed in the thing for which I sent it."[1] Words reveal our thoughts, and together they shape our experiences. When we think of ourselves as healthy, the words we send forth help shape healthy experiences just as we have verbalized them. We have the God-given ability to create our experiences and use our thoughts and words to activate what we desire to create. So if we're going to create, we may as well create what we want rather than what we do not want. It just makes good sense to consciously use the words of a healthy mind to create a healthy body.

Some of the ways we can create and support a healthy mind and body are by speaking words that bless, affirm, and honor our potential to experience wholeness. When we use our words, backed by the power of a prayer-centered consciousness of health and divinely inspired actions, we demonstrate healing of every kind. Even when we experience good health, we should speak words of wholeness to ourselves. Do not wait until a health challenge arises to speak loving words to your body. The whole point of this book is to pray up your life even before tough challenges occur, with the thought that some will be averted and for the ones that do show up, you'll have the strength, faith, and tools to move through them.

Prayer Practice

In your time of prayer, speak affirmative words about your mind and to your body. Speak to every area of your body from the top of your head to the soles of your feet. Visualize yourself healthy in mind, body, and affairs as you speak the words.

Here are some examples, but form your own prayers; they will have more meaning and power for you if you create them especially for your use:

- Focusing your attention on your eyes, say, *"You see clearly without strain. You are the perfect set of eyes for me, and I bless all that you do for me. You see good everywhere and in all people. I love you and appreciate you for helping me see life, love, wisdom, and truth in all my experiences."*

- Focusing your attention on your heart, say, *"Thank you for being a radiating center of love. Thank you for beating the appropriate number of times each moment of my days. Thank you for pumping blood easily through my veins. I bless you as a healthy organ in my body fulfilling the divine purpose for which God appointed you."*

- Focusing inward for your overall health and well-being, say, *"I am grateful for my healthy, attractive, vibrant body. Every cell in my body is healthy, blessed, and radiant. I enjoy my body, and my body enjoys me. Good health is mine now and always."*

- Focusing your attention on the area between your eyes (the third eye) or at the very top of your head (crown chakra), say, *"My mind is in tune with the mind of God. I think clearly; I know what is mine to know. I understand easily and, when divinely inspired, take appropriate spirit-guided action. Spirit easily flows in and through my whole thinking process with wisdom and power. My thoughts are programmed for positive ideas and grand success."*

As you prayerfully affirm positive statements to bless your mind and body, you'll develop the habit of thinking and saying kind things to yourself about yourself. You could even go so far as to write yourself a love note and enjoy being encouraged by your own pleasant view of who you are and what you aspire to become. This will also facilitate being kind to your mind and body in outer ways through positive, healthful lifestyle choices.

14

When a Loved One Dies

<u>Prayer Anchor</u>: "Yea, though I walk through the valley
of the shadow of death, I will fear no evil; For You are
with me; Your rod and Your staff, they comfort me. Surely
goodness and mercy shall follow me All the days of my
life; and I will dwell in the house of the LORD Forever."

Psalms 23:4, 6 (NKJV)

When a loved one leaves our physical presence by way of the transition we call death, we wonder about the experience of death itself and what it means. We wish there was something we could do to rest assured that our loved one is not somewhere hurting, missing us as we are missing him or her. We want to get through our own thoughts of fear and sometimes guilt. We want the pain of loss and separation to subside. We want to know if our loved one is somehow okay in spite of the grief we are feeling.

Psalm 23 is often read at funerals and memorial services. The entire scripture is a powerful prayer that has instilled hope, comfort, and promise in the human heart and mind for thousands of years. It is probably one of the most popular scriptures in the Old Testament. We can pray it on behalf of our loved ones to gain reassurance that they are not alone or afraid. We can pray this prayer to begin our own healing journey through the difficult process we know as grief.

Two verses in the scripture can be particularly comforting to mourning family and friends. Verse 4 can be read to tell us our loved one walked through the valley of the shadow of death and was not afraid of the experience called death. This addresses two concerns we have about death: Does it hurt? Should we be afraid of the experience? If we believe the powerful words of this scripture, then the answer to both questions will be no. We can take some comfort in believing that our loved passed on with such peace that there was no pain and no fear in the moments following that last breath. Regardless to how the death occurred, bodily pain ceases with the shutting down of the physical functions of the body.

The second part of verse 4 addresses our concern for where our loved one has gone. Where did he or she go after leaving our sight? Where is he or she now? The psalmist assures us that wherever we are, God is with us and we are with God. Not only is God with our loved one, but he or she is comforted by God's loving presence, the rod and staff of love and peace. Having made it through the valley of the shadow of death lets us know that our loved one will not linger in death but will pass through it into another dimension of existence. The process of dying then becomes one of making a transition from this dimension to the next; therefore it is a transition and not an end. Whatever plane of existence our loved one has moved on to, he or she is not in pain, not afraid; he or she is comforted and surrounded by God's love and peace.

Verse 6 tells us "goodness and mercy will follow us all the days of our lives." The question for some of us becomes what about life after death? Will goodness and mercy follow my loved one into the next dimension? If we embrace Psalm 23, we can rest assured God's presence never ends, and where God is, there is life.

Of course our questions regarding death and dying will best be answered in the context of our religious or spiritual beliefs. I believe it is natural to bring up the question of eternal life and what that looks like when we are concerned about the fate of our dearly departed loved one. However, I suggest that since the transition we call death is something we will all face at some point, it may be healing to at least consider that a loving God would not bind us in a place where we would suffer eternally.

Verse 6 ends this powerful prayer: "And I will dwell in the house of the Lord forever." Since our loved one is not with us physically, it may be comforting to know he or she is in the house of the Lord.

I believe it is healthy to have questions about life and death, death and dying, birth and eternal life. I've not tried to answer those questions here for you, only to stir up your beliefs for possible confirmation, reconsideration, or more in-depth study.

We owe it to our departed loved one to hold in our minds the best possible thoughts we can toward the transition he or she faces. One of the best things we can do on his or her behalf is to send our love and blessings to them. Through prayer, we can flood our minds with positive thoughts about what this transition from visible to invisible could mean from a spiritual perspective. We can fill the void in our hearts that wants to do something by praying for a peaceful walk into the light, into another dimension of God's care and keeping.

In the process, we will learn what is ours to know from this side of the experience. Through prayer, we have the opportunity to discover that our connection with our loved one is not lost but altered toward greater spiritual understanding, personal growth, and the realization of unending love. As we heal through our own grief, we gain the insight that love "…bears all things, believes all things, hopes all things, endures all things."[1]

Prayer Practice

As soon after the transition is made or as the person is making the transition, light a white candle on his or her behalf. If you have a picture of the person, you may place the candle near the picture.

Begin to pray. Speak the person's name and give thanks to God for a peaceful transition, a healing transition, a spiritual walk into the light of everlasting, divine love. Envision a white light surrounding the person as healing light. Know that on the soul level, whatever healing needs to take place is done.

Say this prayer that I crafted from Psalm 23 on behalf of your loved one in this way: *"Dear _____(name of the person), the Lord God is your shepherd; you shall never again want for anything. You now rest in green pastures of eternal love.*

You are guided on a journey near the still waters of perfect peace, and your soul is restored to wholeness. Your walk into the light confirms for you that God is everywhere present; you are not alone or lonely. Even though you walk through what you once believed was a dark valley called death, you have no fear; now you walk in the light of truth. You feel the rod and staff of love and peace upon your spirit and discover the comfort of true eternal bliss. You find a banquet table laid out before you in the place where there is no knowledge of or idea called an enemy. Your head is anointed with sweet fragrances of various healing oils, and all of life's mysteries fade into nothingness, leaving you to rest in divine perfection."

"Dear _____(name of the person), I rejoice with you for the goodness and mercy that enfolds you now and throughout eternity. I find my own personal joy and comfort in knowing you dwell in the consciousness of eternal love now and forever. Amen!"

Light a candle and pray this prayer once a day for nine days, (nine symbolizes a harmonious ending and time of peaceful completion). Know that as you pray this prayer for your loved one, you are also beginning your healing process.

If at no other time you can think of when you need a spiritual community, it is especially important when mourning the loss of a loved one. In my experience, the people whose lives are devastated to the point of slow or no return from their grief, are those who did not have a spiritual support system to help them grieve. Spiritual counseling, support groups, and prayer are the tools we need to help us move through the grief process with poise and grace. My suggestion: Don't attempt to go through grief alone. Get help and let others pray with you and for you—your loved one would have it no other way.

Part 3

Prayer Practices That
Add Energy and Power

15

The Sweet Smell of Answered Prayer

Prayer Anchor: "Then Noah built an altar to the Lord, and took of every clean animal and of every clean bird, and offered burnt offerings on the altar. And the Lord smelled a soothing aroma. Then the Lord said in his heart, 'I will never again curse the ground...'"

Genesis 8:20–21 (NKJV)

In ancient times, scented oils and fragrant materials were used during religious rituals. There was a belief that the fragrance would attract the attention of God, and the prayer would be favored because of the sweet smell. The Egyptians were supposedly fond of aromatic substances and used them often and generously, particularly in their religious practices. These oils were also used to adorn the body in various kinds of rituals and ceremonies as well.

Aromatherapy as we know it today is the evolution of some early beliefs that there was a connection between scent and health, beauty, sensuality, and certain states of consciousness. I'm sure you have specific scents that evoke certain states of being within you.

For a time, when I was a young girl, I lived with my oldest sister, her husband, and their three children. My father died when I was four years old, and living with my sister was the first time I'd really felt part of a family where a dad was present. Every morning, my sister would make breakfast for her husband and send him off to work at about 5 a.m. So I would wake up to the aroma of coffee, bacon, homemade bread, and sometimes apple cinnamon rolls.

Even today, more than forty years later, when I smell any of these items, it brings a smile to my face as I recall some happy childhood times. The aromas take me back to a time when I felt a deep connection with family, a closeness that I needed at that time in my growth and development.

Our sense of smell can trigger memories, feelings, and emotions as well as activate the mind toward hope and inspiration. We should not underestimate our God-given sense of smell for it has the ability to change our emotional state in a moment. Think about it. Does any particular smell take you back to a happy time or even a sad time?

The above scripture illustrated God as having a change of heart by smelling a pleasing odor, but it is you and I whose mind may be opened up and changed by fragrant aromas.

Certain scents are said to be effective in addressing certain experiences, whether they be mental, physical, or emotional. They can also be used for lifting our spirit. If you are interested in aromatherapy, I would recommend that you do some study on your own and then talk to an aromatherapy practitioner. Unless you are addressing an illness, I suggest you use your nose as your guide. Trying essential oils that are pleasing to you is the best place to start in addition to reading up on the subject.

Here are a few suggestions when using essential oils: Look for good-quality oil. Check the label for the notation "pure essential oil." Before applying oil to a large area of your skin or using it in your bath water, test the oil first with just a drop to assure that it is compatible with your skin.

There are various ways to use scented oils. You may use essential oils on your body, inhale the fragrance from the bottle, put a few drops in a diffuser or an air freshener, add a few drops to your bath water, or try any other uses that you investigate or test out. Some oils may be prepared to be ingested as a tea or with food, but read the instructions on the label carefully.

Some of the common scents that you may enjoy are lavender, peppermint, jasmine, rose, and frankincense. If you are not familiar with aromatherapy, I recommend getting a diffuser and begin by using a few drops of lavender. If you are sensitive to aromas, start using fragrances slowly and in small portions. You may want to experiment with many fragrances before settling on a few that fit your taste.

Prayer Practice

Select a scent that is pleasing to you. Look into the different uses for specific oils to see if there is a fragrance that relates to a particular prayer request you have. For example, if you are feeling stressed, tired, or worried, put a few drops of lavender in your diffuser and then spend some time in silent prayer. If you really want to relax, run a warm bath, put a few drops of lavender in the water, light a lavender-scented candle, and enjoy your silent prayer from your tub. Some good-quality oils may be massaged directly on the skin making them excellent for an increase in the quality of relaxation.

Scented candles are also a good way to help stimulate the sense of smell and can be effective in lifting your emotional state. Combined with other spiritual practices, candles can shift the mood and energy in a room almost immediately.

If you're praying for a perfect mate, you might use rose, cinnamon, or jasmine in your diffuser to lift your receptivity to love. If you want to let your mind flow into a deep meditation, frankincense, sandalwood, or a combination of frankincense and myrrh would be great for this. Use lavender and peppermint for relaxation.

Again, your nose is your best judge, along with a little bit of study. Try many scents until you find a few that you really like. Search for high-quality oils to get the best effect.

As always, set your intention as you are putting your diffuser in place and putting the oil in it. To be most effective, know your desire before using this spiritual practice, as with any others that are mentioned in this book.

When you pray, let your sense of smell support you as you breathe deeply for a few minutes. Center your thoughts on the presence of God within. Always remember that the aroma can support your physical and emotional concentration as you pray, but it is not a substitute for prayer. Begin your prayer and enjoy the sweet smell of it being answered.

16

Prayer and Sacred Symbols

Prayer Anchor: "Then the priests brought in the ark of the covenant of the LORD to its place, into the inner sanctuary of the temple, to the Most Holy Place, under the wings of the cherubim. For the cherubim spread their two wings over the place of the ark, and the cherubim overshadowed the ark and its poles."

1 Kings 8:6–7 (NKJV)

The ark of the covenant was Israel's most sacred religious artifact. The above scripture reveals that it was precious and treated with reverence. It was put in "the most holy place" within the sanctuary and underneath the wings of angels as a protective covering.

The religious practice of having a sacred and holy place specifically set aside for acknowledging God's presence has been handed down to us over the ages. It has given rise to many folks setting up an altar in their homes with personal sacred objects that remind them of God's presence.

Most religions and cultures have their own sacred symbols that have particular meaning and purpose to them, including angels, a picture of Jesus or the Virgin Mary, a crucifix, or a statue of Buddha.

These symbols have their unique meaning in a culture or religion but have meaning on an individual level as well. For this reason, if you are guided to have an altar in your home, you should select the symbols to be placed on that altar according to your own beliefs regarding any objects that you place on it. Each item on your altar should have personal significance. This is an important key to your empowerment when you pray before your altar or when you pray using the sacred symbols from your altar.

Our ideas about what is sacred in our religious and spiritual practices stem from what we learned from our ancestors. As we take charge of our own spiritual education, we gain expanded spiritual knowledge.

Trust yourself with regard to what speaks to you and why. When you select sacred objects to use in your prayer practices, they should have meaning to you and a purpose for which you use them.

Use caution, though. There is danger in having an altar and using sacred objects in our prayer practices. Many battles were fought over the ark of the covenant. Many lives were sacrificed to recapture the ark and get it back to Jerusalem.

That same danger exists for us. Although we may not lose our lives over our sacred objects, we can give away the recognition of our power to an object when we think we must have it in order to feel God's presence. There is always the risk of putting our faith and hope in the object. If this happens, we could experience difficulty becoming consciously aware of God's presence when we are separated from the object. We can find ourselves making a statue of Jesus or the Virgin Mary that which we worship. That is a form of losing ourselves and our spiritual stronghold on truth. A sacred object is not to be worshiped or used as an idol.

So while I say it is an acceptable and helpful practice to have an altar, remember to keep yourself balanced with the use of any symbol—the meaning behind the object can be an important part of your spiritual practice. Let your devotion be to your higher power—God at work in you.

Sacred symbols and objects used properly can help us focus on God's presence within us. We can use them as a means of drawing nearer to our own spiritual and religious beliefs. What we think regarding the objects can support us in feeling God's presence within. The use of sacred symbols and objects can best support our prayer practices when we remember that they are symbols that we may use to acknowledge a much deeper power within us.

Anything you do on the outside has already been done on the inside. So if you choose not to set up an altar for prayer and meditation, set one up in your own mind and visit it on a regular basis. This way wherever you go, you take your altar with you.

If you do decide to set up an altar in your home, be clear on your purpose for having it and why it is important to you. Always use your spiritual understanding to discern what is right for you.

Arrange your altar in a place that is not on public display or in view of anyone who enters your home. If someone does see your altar, it should be because you have invited him or her to do so. Each person's energy is different according to his or her beliefs, which may not be in harmony with yours. "But you, when you pray, go into your room, and when you have shut your door, pray to your Father who is in the secret place; and your Father who sees in secret will reward you openly."[1] Think of your altar as your own private place of prayer.

You may want to look into the Chinese art of feng shui, which is the ancient philosophy of correct placement to maximize the flow of energy in your environment. Using the feng shui principles can help determine which area of your home will be most conducive to prayerful, peaceful meditative energy. You may also use the principles of feng shui to help with where to locate items on your altar.

Regarding where and what to place on your altar, let your intuition guide you. You are always your own best guide as to what is best for you. If you choose the trial and error method, try what you feel may work for you, and see what happens. As you pay attention to your life, you will be able to determine if you are on the right track.

Here are a few general suggestions: Select items carefully to be placed on your altar. They should speak to your personal spiritual beliefs. Do not crowd your altar. More doesn't necessarily mean better. Keep your altar clean. Remember that it is a place for sacred symbols and items you use during your devotional time, such as a Bible or other sacred texts, inspirational works, candles, incense, and aromatherapy essential oils. Add color; white, for example, represents spirituality, purification, and healing. But be guided from within regarding use.

Then, place your sacred objects on the altar, which may include your statues or pictures of goddesses, saints, Jesus, angels, Buddha, the Virgin Mary, loved ones, personal heroes (and she-roes), and whatever feels right to you. It would also be appropriate to place your stones, crystals, prayer beads, etc. if you choose. The important thing is that each item you place has a purpose and a meaning for you.

Prayer Practice

If you choose to set up an altar, make it personal with your preferences and spiritual practices. Remember that your true altar is your inner meeting place with God, and that place is within. You may still choose to have an outer, physical place that you favor for your time of prayer and meditation. The material objects you place there are those you feel will support your inner work.

Your altar should be a place where you feel drawn to pray, meditate, sit in the silence, and have your regular devotional experience. The more you pray up the space, the deeper will be your level of comfort at your altar. Whether you decide to kneel, sit, or stand is your preference, but a consistent habit of prayer at your altar will intensify your sense of internal spiritual harmony while praying there. Your altar and your prayer practices before your altar are personal to your spiritual and religious beliefs. Enjoy the space you have created to acknowledge, honor, and celebrate your relationship with God's presence in you.

17

Light a Candle

Prayer Anchor: "Therefore take heed that the light which is in you is not darkness. If then your whole body is full of light, having no part dark, the whole body will be full of light, as when the bright shining of a lamp gives you light."

Luke 11:35–36 (NKJV)

When we light a candle for the purpose of setting our intention toward prayer, we are reminded that the light of truth, the spark of divinity, is within us. We light the candle to enhance our inner light. If there is any darkness in us (meaning negativity, fear, or worry), the light will chase the darkness away. Lighting a candle can be an affirmation that we do not choose to carry negativity into our time of prayer. As we turn our thoughts to the outer light, all our inner erroneous beliefs are brought into the light of life, love, wisdom, and truth. We symbolically turn on our inner light when we light a candle.

As I have said several times in this book, we should not put our faith in outer symbols, but we may use them to enhance our ability to focus inward. We light a candle and enjoy its beauty, embrace its fragrance, and celebrate the flame it mirrors in us. The flame reflects the light of truth within us and supports us on our inward journey.

On our journey of spiritual evolution, we may find that adopting a spiritual practice as simple as lighting a candle may help to build a consciousness that reminds us of our own inner light. The warmth, beauty and energy we enjoy from the outer light can support the inner comfort, healing and gathering of strength we desire from a prayerful experience.

Scented candles are excellent to use if we choose to engage our sense of smell as part of our prayer experience. Candles come in all kinds of beautiful shapes and sizes, so we may also engage our sense of sight while we enjoy the striking glow of a lit candle.

Then there is color. There are all kinds of theories on the effect that color may have on our emotional state, health, attitude, etc. There are many books written on the subject that provide more information on what color of candle is best for you to burn and when to use particular colors.

Here are a few general guidelines on the selection of candles to use for your spiritual practices:

Color Preferences
- Use red to incite passion; it evokes feelings of love and invigorates a highly stimulating energy.

- Use orange as an attention getter. Its energy inspires: ideas, romance, attraction, beauty, encouragement, and friendship.

- Use yellow for inner joy, feelings of happiness, vitality, inspiration, illumination, and mental clarity.

- Use green for health, tranquility, a sense of meaning and purpose, and prosperity.

- Use blue for inner peace, relaxation, enhanced faith, hope, and an expectation of good.

- Use purple for the feeling of wealth, prosperity, royalty, power, sensuality, and spirituality.

- Use pink for relaxation, calming energy, and drawing on inner beauty; it evokes feelings of love (for self, life, God, and others), intimacy, and romance.

- Use white for clarity, purity, and spiritual power.

Number of Candles to Burn

To determine how many candles to burn at one time, use your own intuition, but be aware that certain numbers of candles may support your intention. Here is a brief guide:

- Burn a single candle for spirituality, leadership, new pursuits and independent issues.

- Burn two candles for companionship and relationship issues

- Burn three candles for creativity, wisdom and guidance issues.

- Burn four candles for order and structure issues.

- Burn five candles for adventure, new opportunities and travel issues.

- Burn six candles for family, love or community issues.

- Burn seven candles for inner growth, self-knowledge and academic pursuits.

- Burn eight candles for prosperity, finances and material possessions.

- Burn nine candles for high level spiritual work, harmonious endings and global issues.

Shapes to Consider

Candles come in many shapes that represent a particular symbolism. You may have seen crucifix-shaped candles or candles made to look like a man or a woman, or heart-shaped candles. You name it, there is great variety available. I suggest that if burning candles is a regular part of your spiritual practice, you will enjoy experimenting with different types and shapes.

Personally, I burn candles almost daily in my spiritual practices. I like the color, fragrance, warm glow of the flame, and symbolism of reflecting my inner light. I find that the tea light candles are convenient, cost-effective, safe, and available in a variety of colors, so this works for me. I use longer-burning candles for various purposes.

For example, as I wrote this section, I burned a pink heart-shaped candle. In my prayer time this morning, I set an intention to be open to the relaxed, soothing, calming effects of divine love in me as I enjoy a day of writing.

Prayer Practice

Decide on your purpose for using a candle in your prayer practice. This will help you select the color, shape, size, and number to burn. Remember to take safety precautions whenever you burn candles.

When you light your candle, mentally set a positive intention. Often, when I perform a wedding ceremony, the couple will elect to light two small tapered candles and jointly light one large candle. The outer representation is that the two people join their lives together as one.

Light your candle, and begin your prayer. Let the outer light be a reminder of your inner light that is waiting to be expressed in and through you in an infinite number of ways. "You are the light of the world."[1]

18

Add Soul-Stirring Music

Prayer Anchor: "Praise Him with the sound of the
trumpet; Praise Him with the lute and harp! Praise Him
with the timbrel and dance; Praise Him with stringed
instruments and flutes! Praise Him with loud cymbals;
Praise Him with clashing cymbals! Let everything that
has breath praise the LORD. Praise the LORD!"

Psalm 150:3–6 (NKJV)

Did you ever hear a piece of music that brought you to tears? Perhaps
you've heard a piece of music that emotionally affected you, evoking
feelings of sadness or joy, or it caused you to want to dance or clap.
Perhaps you've heard music that took you to another place mentally,
and you thought about the past, future, or things imagined.

Music has the ability to reach deep places within us, even when
words cannot. Life itself has a compelling rhythm, and our heart
beats to it. There is a rhythmic celebration going on inside us all the
time. The tune is set to the cadence of life that moves every moment
within us in sweet harmonic communion with God.

Consider adding music to your personal prayer practice from
time to time. Seek out various kinds of music that connect with
your emotional state. Searching for the music that stirs your soul

will be an added blessing. As you put your intention and desire into the search for music, you will be guided to what stirs your heart and lifts your spirit.

Make your specially chosen music part of your daily routine. Use it during times of prayer as well as for background music during your day. Change your musical selection from time to time. The idea is to spend time prayerfully listening to music and to allow it to support your inward journey into times of stillness, silence, and meditation.

If you work in an environment that will allow it, play carefully chosen background music while you work. Many studies have been done on the effects of music on our mood and motivation, so be selective and you'll see positive results.

Prayer Practice

If you already use music to complement your prayer time, that is great. Remember to vary your musical selection from time to time. This will allow you to get the most from this prayer practice. In this way, you are continually open to new opportunities that other musical selections may bring.

If you are new to using music as part of your prayer practice, it can be fun shopping for music that you will enjoy. Ask friends or others in your spiritual community if they have recommendations and then listen to lots of music that uplifts and inspires until you find what stirs your soul. When you hear it, you'll know it—you'll feel it.

Play the music softly in the background as you have your personal prayer time or just be still and listen, allowing the notes of the music to carry you off to wonderful places of joy, peace, relaxation, and love.

One meditation practice you can use is to listen for a particular note in the musical piece and let it carry you off on a meditative journey. Fall into its rhythm and form, letting it carry you through the song. This can be revealing as well as stimulating to your creativity.

Let the music begin!

19

The Use of Incense

Prayer Anchor: "LORD, I cry out to You; Make haste to me! Give ear to my voice when I cry out to You. Let my prayer be set before You as incense, The lifting up of my hands as the evening sacrifice."

Psalm 141:1-2 (NKJV)

In ancient times, incense was used in religious rituals and ceremonies as a symbolic offering of prayer to God. Incense was also burned each morning and evening as a demonstration of continued devotion to God.

When incense is burned, the white smoke that travels upward is symbolic of a phrase you may have heard: "sending up prayers to God." It was believed that the white smoke and the fragrant smell called God's attention to the prayers. "Now at the time of the incense offering, the whole assembly of the people was praying outside."[1]

In the prayer anchor above, David asks for a quick response. He states that he wants his prayer to have the kind of attention as if he were burning incense in God's presence.

As an empowering spiritual practice, today when we light our incense and focus on God within, we enjoy the fragrant smell and set our mind toward the idea of answered prayer. We watch the white smoke go up as a symbol of taking our thoughts higher and connecting with God on a personal and sacred level. Our emotional state can be lifted to bring about a more receptive frame of mind.

When selecting incense, you will want to be attracted to the smell. You should find it pleasing in order to get the full effect of burning it during your time of prayer. Do not underestimate the power of your sense of smell. Certain fragrances have the ability to arouse various emotions in us. In selecting incense, you want to attract a fragrance that arouses uplifting emotions for you.

In ancient times, only the priest could light incense in the temple. It was considered a sacred act and a holy ritual, as it symbolized approaching God with a prayer. For this reason, I suggest that you keep the act of incense lighting sacred. Wash your hands before handling the incense. It is symbolic that you are not holding onto any negativity as you set your conscious intention toward God and that you consider it part of your prayer. When you light your incense, keep your thoughts toward God, life, beauty, love, wisdom, etc. There should be no negative thinking when lighting your incense; in fact, intentionally set your mind on godly ideas.

Learn about the various incense fragrances. Incense has different uses according to its effect on our sense of smell and the energy that it holds. Many incense fragrances are also available in oil form. Some of my personal favorites are frankincense, frankincense combined with myrrh, lavender, sandalwood, orange, orange blossom, rose, bergamot, and sage. You can go strictly by the smell, or you can go a little deeper by studying the various mystical properties attributed to certain kinds of incense. Experiment until you find what works for you.

Prayer Practice

Before you begin your prayer, wash your hands and face if possible, this is to prepare yourself physically for the sacred act of prayer. The simple act of cleansing before prayer establishes a sense of reverence for your meeting with God in prayer. Begin your mental preparation by setting an intention to clear your mind of any negativity. The idea here is to approach the lighting of the incense as a sacred act for the holy purpose of prayer. Put your mind on some divine idea (such as love, peace, harmony, joy, beauty, faith, etc.) as you light your incense.

When you light the incense, use an incense holder to catch the ashes as it burns. Then begin your time of prayer.

Enjoy the fragrance from the incense. Imagine that the incense gives your prayers power because of how you are affected by your sense of smell and your intentions for answered prayer. You may even want to pattern your prayer after David's: *"I call upon you, O Lord; come quickly to me; give ear to my voice when I call to you. Let my prayer be counted as incense before you, and the lifting up of my hands as an evening sacrifice."*[2]

When your prayer is complete and the incense is burned, clean up the ashes and discard them. With these actions you affirm *"It is done!"* As you toss the ashes away, say aloud, *"Amen!"*

20

Using Precious Stones

Prayer Anchor: "And he made the breastplate, artistically woven like the workmanship of the ephod, of gold, blue, purple, and scarlet thread, and of fine woven linen. They made the breastplate square by doubling it; a span was its length and a span its width when doubled. And they set in it four rows of stones: a row with a sardius, a topaz, and an emerald was the first row; the second row, a turquoise, a sapphire, and a diamond; the third row, a jacinth, an agate, and an amethyst; the fourth row, a beryl, an onyx, and a jasper. They were enclosed in settings of gold in their mountings."

Exodus 39:8–13 (NKJV)

In the Bible, precious stones are mentioned in numerous places for various purposes. A headpiece made of precious stone was placed on David's head after one of his conquests. David made a generous donation to the temple that his son, Solomon, was to build that included many precious stones. When Solomon finished building the temple, he had it adorned with precious stones. The Queen of Sheba brought precious stones to Solomon as a gift that he might share his wisdom with her.

In the books of Exodus and Revelation, the names of twelve precious stones are revealed. In Revelation, the stones were used as a foundation around the Temple of Jerusalem. In Exodus, the stones were used to adorn the breast piece worn by the priests. These two Biblical references have ten of the twelve stones in common. The number 12 is significant because it stands for wholeness and perfection.

In ancient times, very specific uses were ascribed to certain precious stones and they were believed to have mystical powers to support the intended use. In some instances, they were believed to ward off evil and negativity and to provide protection from enemies. Precious stones also implied great wealth, especially since many of the precious stones spoken of in the scriptures were rare and valuable, as many of them still are today.

Whether precious stones actually carry mystical energy could be debated. However, many of our ancestors believed these stones had energies that would protect, heal, and bring favorable conditions and good fortune, and it seemed to work for them.

I enjoy the beauty of precious stones. Some of them can be easily acquired at reasonable prices. I am one of those people who is open to the possibility that stones from the earth may carry energy. I also know that what we believe has great power. So, if we believe that this energy can be activated through prayer and meditation to help awaken our inner potential that will be our experience.

However, I am not suggesting that we give away our powerful ability to draw into our lives what we desire by relying on a stone to deliver it to us. The twenty-eighth chapter of Job speaks of many precious stones as having great value but makes the point that they are not the source of God's wisdom.

If you are interested in precious stones for use in spiritual work, ceremonies, or to wear for their beauty, study the types of stones to be used for the purposes of your particular interest.

Many books describe the energy attributed to various stones. For example, the sapphire mentioned in Exodus as one of the twelve stones on the priest's breastplate and in Revelation as adorning the temple in the coming age is said to have the energy of wisdom, peace, love, power, and healing.

If you desire to draw on the energy of precious stones in your time of prayer, here are my suggestions: After you have done your own study of the type of stone you want to use, thoroughly cleanse the stone to reset its energy and release any negative energy from others who may have handled it previously. Do this by soaking the stone in water and sea salt for at least twenty-four hours; while three days is better, seven days is best—the longer the cleansing period, the deeper the cleaning. Salt is used since it is one of the earth's oldest minerals and has long been used for purification. Salt derived from seawater brings to the cleansing process many of the mystical properties of the ocean. You may also set the stone outside to gather energy from the sun.

Take time to study the energy of the stones you choose. Set your own intentions for the stones, and follow your inner guidance when it comes to using them. You are your own best guide for what is best for you. Your selection process may be that you like the color or that you are intuitively drawn to a particular stone.

Prayer Practice

During your time of prayer or meditation, clasp your stone in your hands and consciously set your mind on what you desire. Whatever stone you choose to use should be in alignment with your prayerful desire. For example, you might use the sapphire if your prayer is related to the energy of wisdom, peace, love, power, or healing.

As you hold your stone, think only positive thoughts about your prayer desire. You may work with your stone on a daily basis if you have a particular prayer request. Set a length of time for consistent use of the stone, such as twelve, or forty days. After that, take a break, cleanse the stone, and begin using it again when you're ready.

Some suggestions for stones to use have been mentioned in the scriptures quoted above. Some of my personal favorites are emerald, amethyst, carnelian, beryl, chrysolite (which you'll find as peridot), and sapphire. While I like sapphires, I find them more expensive than I prefer to pay for a meditation stone. Some of my other personal favorites not listed in the above scripture are rose quartz, lapis lazuli, chrysoprase, chrysocolla, tiger's eye, topaz, amber, and jade. Check them out and enjoy! If you like jewelry, these stones make excellent pieces to wear for their beauty and the uplifting feeling you may experience when wearing a work of art made from the earth.

But I can't say this enough: your power is not in a stone. Using the stone may help you focus your mind on your desire, and once you get your desire clearly in mind, you'll bring it into manifestation by the power of God at work in and through you.

21

Keep a Journal

I have kept a personal journal continuously for the last thirty years and sporadically when I was a child. In addition to the therapeutic benefits of writing out my thoughts, feelings, and prayers, I find great comfort having a written record of major events (and not-so-major events) I have experienced.

I journal regularly as part of my spiritual practice. I keep at least two journals simultaneously: my gratitude journal, which I write in a few times each week, and a daily journal. Since I am a journaler, I keep my writing interesting by changing the theme of my journals from time to time. For example, in addition to my gratitude journal, I have maintained journals of prayer, angels, prosperity, pray until something happens, and love and romance, among others. The beauty of journaling is that you can create whatever works for your taste, desire, and interest.

When journaling, I write my hopes, goals, dreams, prayers and new ideas that come to me. For many years, I used a structured journal that prompted me to write my goals for the year, month, week, and day. There was a place to make a covenant with God and to keep a daily gratitude list. It was a fun and effective way to work on the practical aspects of my life as well as my spiritual growth and development.

In my journal, I give myself permission to be who I am. I write what my thoughts are at the time. I write affirmations, denials, prayers, inspirational quotes, and scriptures to help me work with whatever I am feeling and thinking. It has been a blessing for me to have a private place where I can go and share whatever is on my mind and heart without fear of judgment or criticism. I don't make it a practice of criticizing myself in my journal. In my journaling, I accept myself as I am. I use my journal to support my personal growth, help me stay focused on my desire to be the best me I can, and infuse spiritual inspiration into my day.

As a spiritual tool, I love having what I call a written journey of my faith in God. I can read back over my entries and see how my faith has deepened over the years, whereas, while in the midst of daily living, I did not recognize my spiritual progress. There have been times I have been so busy with my daily routine, schedule, and to-do list that I missed God's answers to my prayers. It was not until I looked back over my journal that I was able to see clearly and, in my own handwriting, God's answer to my prayers.

I have my journals from the last twenty-five years, and occasionally I will go back and see where I was in consciousness and discover how far I have come. I remember looking back to one of my earlier journals and finding an entry that read, "Dear God, I think I'm going to die." As I read on, a problem was described in great detail, and obviously it was from a place of great pain. I continued to read through the journal, and four months after the entry, I found a declaration of praise and celebration. The problem that had devastated me so deeply four months earlier had become a cause for gratitude, appreciation, and joy.

I like remembering that and similar stories about my journey. It reminds me that even if it seems like there is no answer and no hope, if I hang on and remain steadfast in my prayer practices, the situation will not only pass, but there will again be cause for celebration. This is the greatest value I find in keeping a journal as a regular spiritual practice. I suspect as long as I am able to write, I will have one.

In my gratitude journal, sometimes I'll make a list of things for which I am grateful. Other times, I may write a gratitude letter to God as a reminder of how blessed my life really is. Sometimes I write a gratitude letter to myself, thanking me for all I do to make my life what God wants it to be. And there are times when I write gratitude letters to other people as a way of being grateful for that person in my life. While I don't send the letter, sometimes I am prompted to give that person a call within the next day or two.

My gratitude journal entries are also a joy to review to get a special lift. I get to see how my level of gratitude has grown and be reminded of the good that I enjoy.

Journaling can also be fun for those of us who do it regularly. I sometimes decorate my journals. I enjoy using different colored pens and types of writing instruments. I may even draw a picture or tape a picture from a magazine in my journal or put a prayer card that really speaks to me in it. I let my journal be an active part of my spiritual practice.

One reason people say they don't keep a personal journal is privacy. To be totally (and sometimes brutally) honest in your journal, you must be comfortable that no one will read your entries but you. Do what you must to keep your journal private. This way you can feel free to write your true feelings, thoughts, and the inspiration from spirit that will be revealed. This kind of honesty is what enhances the benefits of journaling. "Thus speaks the LORD God of Israel, saying: 'Write in a book for yourself all the words that I have spoken to you.'"[1]

I highly recommend adding journaling to your spiritual practice if you are not already doing so.

Prayer Practice

Purchase a journal or a notebook for your private use. Decide what your journal will be used for and use it only for that purpose, not to write down grocery lists or phone numbers, too. Write whatever you want as often as you want. However, you will gain the most by making your journal a consistent part of your spiritual work.

On the days that you choose not to write in your journal, review something you have already written. You'll be amazed at how inspired you are by your previous entries.

- Have a secure place to keep your journal so that your privacy will not be compromised by visitors or others in your household.

- Date each entry in your journal. This will help when you look back over what you've done and try to identify some areas of personal growth.

- Decide if you will use one journal or multiple journals for specific purposes.

- There is a process I call the repetition method in journaling where you write your prayer desire for a specific number of times each day until you feel that the prayer has been recorded in your subconscious. For example you would write a prayer, positive statement or scripture twelve, twenty-one, forty or as many times as you feel it will help to anchor the idea within; do this exercise daily until you reach a level of inner satisfaction with what you have written. Repetition helps get the thoughts and prayers into our consciousness, and that is the point where we draw the experience for which we are praying into manifestation.

If you want to keep journals for specific topics or subjects, here are a few suggestions:

Prayer journal: In this type of journal, you will write your prayers. They can be your own specific prayers, or you can include prayers from scriptures or other inspirational writings that adequately describe your desire.

Gratitude journal: If you are new to journaling and just want to try it for a time, I would recommend starting with a gratitude journal. Make a commitment to write in the journal every day at least ten things for which you are grateful. No entry is too small. In fact, be sure to include the "smaller" things in life, for these are less obvious yet offer much to be grateful for.

Goals journal: Here you will write about the goals you want to achieve. Write your goals as affirmative statements, and write about how you will achieve them. Be sure to write about your progress as you work on your goals. You may want to add inspirational scriptures or quotes that inspire your focused commitment to what you desire to achieve.

Angel journal: If you like angels, you may enjoy keeping this type of journal. Write daily to your guardian angel for support in whatever you are working on. You may also write to the guardian angel of loved ones to thank them for their support or to angels who serve God for specific purposes. Consider writing to the angel of prosperity, health, or love and romance, for example. However, remember that angels, as messengers of God, can support only the good that God provides. So do not worship angels, but consider them as helpers.

Inspirational journal: In this type of journal, write whatever inspires you. This could be scriptures, other sacred texts, quotes, lyrics to songs, etc.

Pray until something happens journal: If you are working on one or more specific prayer desires that you intend to stay with until you received some kind of guidance regarding them, this is the journal for you. Write out your prayer desires daily and then spend time visualizing them as a reality. Include regular gratitude statements to help prepare your mind to receive your blessings.

Prosperity journal: Write out your desire for the level of prosperity that you want to achieve and sustain. Read works on prosperity from many sources, and write your thoughts, goals, dreams, and desires based on what you read. Write prosperity scriptures and statements that support your intention. Write how you will achieve and work toward the level of prosperity you desire. Some examples of prosperity scriptures you may use are Psalm 23:1, Psalm 118:25, and Deuteronomy 8:18.

Health journal: Write the desire you have for your health. Make a study of what you intend for your mind, body, and spirit. Write your own words as well of the words of others that inspire and support the level of health you desire. Some examples of health scriptures include Proverbs 4:23, 1 Corinthians 3:16, and Romans 12:2. **Love and romance journal:** If love and romance is your focus, this type of journal will be a blessing. Write what you want to achieve. Read Chapter 42 of this book and then incorporate those ideas into this type of journal. Additionally, read other books on relationships that offer suggestions on what you may do to ready yourself for your desire. Write in your journal anything that inspires you to be more loving of yourself and others. Some examples of scriptures on love are 1 Corinthians 13, 1 John 4:16, Psalm 119:41, and 1 Timothy 1:5. Fortunately, much has been written on the subject of love. Study love, write about love in your journal, and then practice with a sincere heart being more loving.

Remember to record your blessings and the outcomes of what you write about in your journal. Your personal testimonies will strengthen your faith and provide great encouragement. There are many possibilities for journaling so be creative and have fun. The important thing to remember is that your journal can be an important tool for your spiritual journey. Try it, and discover your own appreciation for its benefits.

22

Hold a Prayer Vigil

Prayer Anchor: "And Cornelius said, 'Four days ago, about this hour, I was keeping the ninth hour of prayer in my house; and behold, a man stood before me in bright apparel, saying, "Cornelius, your prayer has been heard and your alms have been remembered before God".'"

Acts 10:30–31 (RSV)

Cornelius was "keeping the ninth hour of prayer." This tells us he was in a time of focused, committed prayer and, in the ninth hour, he received a response. A prayer vigil is a commitment to pray for a certain length of time—hours, days, or even months. The vigil is usually kept regarding a specific matter.

A prayer vigil is another way to persist in praying for what we desire to manifest. This entire book is about the many things we can do to spend more time in conscious communion with the presence of God within us. The idea of a vigil is to keep our thoughts centered for an extended time period on what we desire. The more we are focused on our desire, the closer we are to manifesting it—or something better. When we pray with persistence, we build an inner stamina that will draw to us what we are praying to demonstrate or whatever is for our highest good.

The secret to successful prayer is to do it. The secret to really successful prayer is to do it more. In the book of Acts, we discover that Cornelius already had a good prayer life. We are told in a previous scripture that he prayed constantly. This nine-hour prayer vigil was probably normal for him—that is to say, it was a regular part of his spiritual practice. His consistency brought results. The more we build a consciousness of prayer, the more we can expect to get results—and in some instances, expedient results.

A prayer vigil is usually done when we have some matter before us that causes us to believe it will take a little more prayer energy than our normal prayer practice. We may be aware that a deeper change of consciousness is necessary and therefore more time in prayer is required. These are the kind of challenges we take to a prayer vigil. Perhaps we have experienced obstacles or concerns that appear beyond our ability to solve. A heart and mind focused on our trust and faith in God will bring the answers we seek.

Many people overlook a prayer vigil as a possible solution to their desires. First of all, a prayer vigil requires a commitment to our desire and a commitment of our time. When we pray, many of us want God to simply give us what we want immediately with little of our own investment of time and effort. Cornelius received what seemed like an immediate answer to his prayer. But do not forget this was after nine hours of prayer, not to mention a prayer consciousness he had developed over time from praying constantly.

The act of a prayer vigil suggests our own willingness to contribute to the solution. In a prayer vigil, we invest our time, energy, and mind power to receive the rich dividends of God's promises. Have you ever heard it said, "God helps those who help themselves"? When we spend more time in conscious, mind-focused prayer, we are in fact helping God help us.

If we are not willing to put in the time to condition our mind so that we discover, embrace, and accept God's answer to our prayer, the question we should ask ourselves is, "Do I really want God's answer?" We should become still and interrogate ourselves on this question: "Am I really committed to doing what it takes to have God reveal the answer to my prayer?"

A prayer vigil will take us deeper within ourselves to discover God's answer, which may be different from the answer we have in mind. This, too, may be part of our hesitancy in performing a prayer vigil. If in a one-time prayer we could tell God what we want, we'd gladly move on to other things. However, if we repeatedly pray our prayer with the sincerity of consistency, we may discover God's will for us is a bit different from what we had in mind, and yes, sometimes not what we consciously want. Therefore, a prayer vigil requires trust and faith in God's response to our desire.

Some years ago, I held a prayer vigil asking God's guidance for my career. I had a business that was getting by but was not prospering at the level that I desired. I thought that with a prayer vigil, God would make a way for some new business or perhaps give me some marketing strategies I could use. I prayed the same prayers three times a day for seven days. On the morning of the eighth day, I received an answer that was so unexpected, it left me taken aback. I received an answer that meant I was to close my business completely and move to Kansas City, Missouri.

The answer was so far from what I was consciously thinking that I knew it had to be God's answer for me. Yet I immediately began thinking of the excuses for why I could not do this "far out" thing, such as I had a four-year-old son; I'd be a single parent without the extended family support I was accustomed to; I had a business that was at least paying the bills; if I gave my business a little more, I was sure it would grow; I didn't know anyone in Kansas City; and I'd be moving away from all my friends. The list was long. I let the excuses go on for about two hours. I finally realized that I could not dismiss what I had been given. It was God's answer to the prayer I had initiated and, as crazy as it sounded at the time, I had to do as I was guided.

Four months later, I moved to Kansas City. The decision changed my life beyond what I could have ever dreamed. And I have never regretted listening to that still, small voice that revealed itself in me on June 22, 1989, in response to my prayer vigil: "Move to Kansas City."

A prayer vigil is a good test we can give ourselves to discover our level of desire for God's answer to our prayer. If we don't really have a firm desire for the divine answer to our prayer, it makes no difference whether we receive it—and we won't have the consciousness to do right by what we receive or the consciousness to hold on to it.

If I had come to the decision to move to Kansas City by any other means than through my sincere, consistent prayer, I don't know that I would have had the inner strength to follow it through. From a human standpoint, the list of obstacles was insurmountable. Personally, I would have given up after the first few "Are you crazy?" remarks I received from my friends and family. But as I began taking the steps to make the move, the obstacles fell aside like a series of dominos. Channels opened up that I did not even know existed. Because I was prayed up, the answer was revealed to me, and I could receive it and accept it. My choice to make the move was God given, and therefore the path of its manifestation was God driven. In my prayer vigil, one of the scriptures I used was the Lord's Prayer. By repeatedly affirming "Thy will be done," I had come to a place of total surrender.

If your prayer desire is immediate, you may want to stick to a nine-hour vigil or hours in increments of nine. Let the time and the intensity of your prayer desire help decide on the length. An example of the kind of situation that would fit an hourly vigil would be if a loved one was in an emergency surgery situation. You would want to begin your vigil before the actual surgery and go through at least the beginning stages of recovery.

Otherwise, a nine-hour measure of time is sufficient, for it can be very powerful. Keep in mind that the length of the vigil makes God no more attentive to your prayer than if you prayed it once and stopped. Your prayer is not to change God or to win God's favor. Your consistent time in prayer will make you and those for whom you pray more receptive to the answer and ready to receive God's will. For this reason, if you are praying a vigil for someone else, if it is possible, have them join in the prayer with you.

If time is not of the essence, you may choose to spread out your prayer vigil over several days. I have used vigils of three, seven, nine, twenty-one (the power of the number seven magnified by three), and forty days with success. I suggest these numbers because the ancients believed they have sacred meaning; you will see them used frequently throughout the scriptures.

If you do decide to conduct a prayer vigil, know that what we call divine intervention reveals itself to a consciousness that is prayed up to receive answers, guidance, and solutions. The power of Spirit in action is always moving us toward our highest good and is always at work on our behalf.

Prayer Practice

To Start

- Spend the time you need to determine your desire.

- Write out your prayer desire so that you will affirm it accurately each time you pray during your vigil.

- Decide if the length of your prayer vigil will be over several hours, days, or months. Then *commit* to this time period. There is great power in your willingness to make a commitment.

- Select a scripture that you feel speaks to your prayer desire. Some scriptures are powerful and can help you to go deep within yourself to do the prayer work needed for your desire. My general recommendation would be any of the prayer anchors in this book.

Set a Time

If you are doing a nine-hour vigil, you will pray at the same time once every hour for nine consecutive hours. If you are praying over several days, decide on the hour(s) you will pray. Be consistent with the time throughout your vigil.

Let's say you decide to do a seven-day prayer vigil. Here are some examples for how you could structure your vigil:

- You could pray at 6:30 a.m. every day for seven days.

- You could select a specific time to pray in the morning and then have a specific time in the evening, like 6:30 a.m. and 9:00 p.m. for each of the seven days.

- You could pray three times a day for the seven days, something like 6:30 a.m., 12:00 p.m., and 9:30 p.m.

- You could elect to pray several times in one sitting over each of the seven days. In this case, you would affirm your prayer desire (step 4 below) three times or however many times you decide. The point is decide on the number in advance and be consistent throughout your vigil. Your desire will be supported by your willingness to make a commitment and to stick to it.

Let your intuition be your guide with these choices.

What to pray

1. Begin your prayer time with silence. Just a minute or two may be sufficient. You are turning your attention away from the outside to the inside.

2. Read the Lord's Prayer aloud from your Bible. Whenever possible, and when you are working with a scripture, read it from your Bible. There is a subliminal message of sincerity and humility when you hold a Bible in your hand from which to pray, read, or study.

3. Read aloud the scripture you have selected specifically for your prayer vigil.

4. Using a scripture verse stated in the first person, or an affirmation that draws you inward (the scriptural passage does not have to be from the Lord's Prayer or the scripture you selected), clearly state the prayer desire you have written with your attention focused within.

Here are some examples of how that might sound:

- *"For God alone my soul waits in silence;*[1] *and I see myself healthy and whole."*

- *"The Kingdom of God is within*[2] *me. I am guided to my right and perfect employment."*

- *"The Lord is my shepherd; I shall not want.*[3] *All my needs are abundantly met."*

- *"Thy kingdom come. Thy will be done.*[4] *Divine answers are revealed to me regarding my relationship with _____."*

If you are praying for someone else, use the scripture directed toward the person and include his or her name: *"_____ (person's name), Christ in you is your hope of glory. You are healthy and whole."*

Carefully choose what speaks to you and design the prayer that suits you.

5. Make a statement of thanks that reveals your trust in God and your gratitude for whatever is the divine outcome. "Rejoice always, pray without ceasing, give thanks in all circumstances; for this is the will of God in Christ Jesus for you."[5] For example,

you could say, "*I celebrate the divine answer to my prayer. As I continue to hold my prayer desire in my heart, I give thanks, knowing God's will is done.*"

6. End your vigil on the final session with something like, "*Holy Spirit, I leave my prayer desire and the answer in your hands.*"

Release the prayer and any concerns for the outcome. Pay attention to what happens in the coming days. Surely you will notice something has happened. But remember that you have placed the situation in God's hands, so leave it there. Let divine order unfold. If you get anxious, say an affirmation such as "*I trust God to reveal the divine outcome to my prayer*"—and then do it.

Part 4

Prayer Practices to Help Clear Away Obstacles

23

Healing Waters

Prayer Anchor: "And Elisha sent a messenger to him, saying, 'Go and wash in the Jordan seven times, and your flesh shall be restored to you, and you shall be clean.'"

2 Kings 5:10 (NKJV)

In the scriptures and many sacred writings, water has been used as a means of healing. Holy men and women have used water in the spiritual cleansings, healing ceremonies, and religious rituals they have performed throughout the ages. Today, many still believe that God's power is active as a healing agent in what is called holy water, or water that is used to heal and bless others.

People have always had a close relationship with water. We have always known it is important to our survival. The earth is made up of nearly 80 percent water. Our bodies are made up of about 70 percent water. We've been told in one form or another that we should drink six to eight glasses of water per day to stay healthy. And we all know the importance of water for personal hygiene. We cannot deny that water and its value have great meaning to our overall well-being.

In our prayer anchor, Elisha tells Naaman to wash in the Jordan River seven times as a cure for his leprosy. Although reluctant, Naaman does as Elisha instructed and his leprosy disappears. Naaman's skin is not only healed, but the scripture says that "...and his flesh was restored like the flesh of a little child, and he was clean."[1]

In the ninth chapter of the gospel according to John, Jesus heals a man who was born blind. He made mud and spread it on the man's eyes, "And He said to him, 'Go, wash in the pool of Siloam' (which is translated, Sent). So he went and washed, and came back seeing."[2] The man did as Jesus instructed him, and the man's sight was restored.

Let us not overlook that Jesus insisted on being baptized in water by John the Baptist. "I baptize you with water for repentance..."[3] Repent means "to change one's mind." When we pray, we are affirming a desire to change our mind from whatever we are experiencing to embrace whatever we desire to experience. Every prayer requires us to change our mind.

One way we may assist with such change is through spiritual cleansing. In this process, we repent or rid ourselves of any negative or erroneous beliefs, and that's where water or the idea symbolized by the use of water comes in. Water represents cleansing. Whether we are immersed in it, such as in a baptism, or whether we wash in a pool of it or have some sprinkled over us, we still must change our mind.

Water alone cannot change someone's mind. However, using water along with prayer, can help remove mental and emotional obstacles. While Jesus asked John to baptize him with water, Jesus never used water to baptize others but he did recommend water to assist with healings, such as with the man he told to go and wash in the pool at Siloam.

Most of us will admit that after a long, stressful day at work, a warm bubble bath can help us relax. Listening to the crashing waves of water from the ocean can help calm an anxious mind, and none of us would dispute how a cool drink of water on a hot summer day can quench our thirst in a way that no other liquid can. Let's face it—there is something about water that we need, enjoy, and appreciate. When it comes to our health and well-being, the value we gain from water must not be overlooked in our overall plan for physical, emotional, mental, and spiritual well-being.

A spiritual bath for the purpose of mental and emotional cleansing can help prepare us to receive prayerful thoughts and words so that healing can take place on all levels of being. Combined with prayer, what might otherwise be a relaxing time in the bathtub becomes a process of clearing out mental blockages that have delayed attracting the good we desire. The healing qualities of water engaged with the body aid in calming the inner spirit. A calm, relaxed spirit is open, receptive, and ready to accept the words of an earnest prayer.

Prayer Practice

Determine your specific prayer request. Write it on a piece of paper. Find a scripture or inspirational reading that is related to your desire.

Shower before taking your spiritual bath. A spiritual bath is not for the purpose of cleaning the physical body but a practice in which we come already physically relieved of the grime and dirt collected on the body during the normal course of the day. Do not use the same water for your spiritual bath that you used to clean your physical body.

Clean the tub after your shower.

Prepare your bath water. If you have a particular ingredient that you like to use for spiritual bathing purposes, feel free to use it. Many health or New Age specialty stores sell packaged bath crystals, herbs, and products that are nourishing to the body and may be used to address specific prayers. Customize your bath to make it suitable for you.

Here are a few of my favorites:

- Add two cups of hyssop tea to warm, running bath water. Hyssop is mentioned in the Bible for cleansing and healing. Or,

- Combine the following in a bowl: two cups of distilled water, one cup of baking soda, one-half cup of Epsom salt, one tablespoon of sea salt, and three drops of lavender essential oil. Mix well and then pour this mixture in the tub under the warm, running water. (Test these ingredients on your skin before using them for a bath). Or,

- Slice a few cucumbers in a glass bowl and pour three cups of distilled water over them. Refrigerate for six hours as the water takes on the nutrients from the cucumbers. Remove the cucumbers and pour the cucumber water under warm, running water for your bath.

Now that your bath is ready, stand in front of the tub and recite aloud your scripture or sacred reading three times. A spiritual bath is a great time to exercise other prayer practices, such as lighting a candle, using incense, and playing soft music in the background. While this is a prayer experience, it is okay to enjoy it.

Get into the tub. Let the water soothe you, support your healing, and lift your spirit. Remember to put your reading and your written prayer request close by so that you may reach it without getting out of the tub.

Begin applying the water to your body. You may use a container or your hands to scoop and then pour water on yourself or apply it with a clean cloth (preferably one that has never been used before or only used for your spiritual bathing). You will apply the water to all areas of your body, not scrubbing but gently applying the water.

Next, recall your reading and begin to concentrate on it. You may stop applying the water to your body to reread your reading and just relax for a time. The main thing is to keep your mind occupied with your reading as a means of clearing it completely before you make your prayer request. If you can totally immerse yourself in the water, do so seven times. If a complete immersion of your head is not desirable, immerse your face. Your bath should be complete in ten to fifteen minutes.

Just before getting out of the tub, read your prayer request aloud three times. Then exit the tub. Pat yourself dry and get dressed. Do not think about your prayer request for twenty-four hours, this is your opportunity to trust that your prayer has been heard. If you need to think about something, think about your reading.

This bath is best just before going to bed because you will feel relaxed in mind and body. While you are asleep, your subconscious mind will be working on the prayer desire you have given it.

Place your written prayer request somewhere close so that after twenty-four hours you may see it and read it daily until you are satisfied that something has changed in you as a result of your prayer.

24

'Dear God' Letters

Prayer Anchor: "Write the things which you
have seen, and the things which are, and the
things which will take place after this."

Revelation 1:19 (NKJV)

This prayer anchor tells us to write. Write about our experiences,
write about the way things are, and write about what we desire to
take place. Great healings can occur when we are open and honest
with ourselves and God. When we are not honest with others, we
block the potential for intimacy, closeness, and true friendship.
However, when we are not honest with ourselves, about, ourselves,
we miss an opportunity to grow, heal, and prosper. Writing provides
a gentle way of being honest about where we are and where we
want to go.

I'll speak to writing two kinds of letters; both letters are
addressed "Dear God." The first type of letter involves simply
writing whatever is in your heart. This is how we "write what we
have seen and what is." Here you are writing a letter as you would
to a dear friend or a loving parent with whom you could share your
most intimate secrets without fear of being judged, criticized, or
shamed by a set of *shoulds*.

This kind of letter opens us up to reveal those things for which our minds and hearts may have no other safe outlet. We may have close friends and family, but still, some things we may choose not to share except with God. In writing this kind of letter, we give ourselves an opportunity to express our intimate feelings and thoughts for our own personal assessment and to feel the safe haven of a compassionate loving God. The letter is not written out of weakness. This kind of letter is written to gain the inner strength that comes with expressed honesty for individual growth and spiritual development.

The second type of letter involves focusing on what we desire to manifest for ourselves. In some spiritual centers or churches, this type of letter is prepared on New Year's Eve as a way of setting an intention for the coming year—"the things which will take place after this." As a result of time spent in prayer, we write the letter and open ourselves to demonstrations of answered prayer. This kind of letter can be written any time we desire to bring clarity to our prayerful desires.

The most important thing in writing either of these letters is to be prayerful and write from the heart. Whatever issues are in your life, your heart can lead the way to solving, clarifying, prospering, or healing any situation. Writing is a very effective method for expressing what is in our hearts. "Keep your heart with all vigilance; for from it flow the springs of life."[1]

Prayer Practice

Decide on the purpose of your letter and the type of letter you will write. Then settle into your time of prayer in the way that works for you. Your goal is to move into a consciousness centered on God within. Prepare to use affirmations, a sacred reading, or any of the prayer practices in this book in coordination with your writing.

Ask that you be guided from within while writing so you can express what is in your heart and mind. Bless your pen and paper before you begin to write. Sit in silent meditation for a time, listening inwardly. Address your letter and then write, write, write. Do not judge or criticize yourself as you write—this will allow you to write with deep sincerity.

Sometimes using an outer symbol can help focus your attention and keep you centered in love, life, wisdom, peace, etc. I have a red heart that I sometimes like to hold in my hand just as a reminder that I want to be guided by divine love within, as I write.

Set your intention to enjoy the writing experience as a prayer. Relax and let Spirit reveal to you what to write.

When you have written all that you desire, read what you have written for clarity and assessment. Make changes and adjustments where you desire. Note any revelations. If you find some, they may be addressed by this or other prayer practices in this book.

If you write the first type of letter, place it in a sealed envelope. Hold it in your hands and state your prayer desire regarding what you have written. Place the envelope in your Bible on a particular scripture that speaks to you. If you don't have a scripture that you particularly feel guided to, use one of these: The Lord's Prayer, Psalm 23, or 1 Corinthians 13.

Set a time period for letting the letter rest on your chosen scripture (three, seven, nine, twelve, twenty-one, or forty days). Write the date on the envelope. After your specified time period has expired, burn the envelope as a symbol of releasing your prayer into the ethers and sending it forth to continue working on your behalf. As you watch the fire consume your desires written in your letter, know that your prayer has been answered and all is well. Remember to take safety precautions when you burn your letter.

If you write the second type of letter, place it in a self-addressed stamped envelope. You may hold it for a particular time period (three, seven, nine, twelve, twenty-one, or forty days; six months; or one year) on a scripture in your Bible and then mail it to yourself. You may also place the letter in a special place in your home—for example, on your altar. The idea is to let the faith, strength, hope, and imagination you demonstrated in putting your desires in writing become a living reality. Open the letter at the appointed time and remember to celebrate your demonstrations. After you feel complete with the letter you may burn it. The churches or centers that make this process part of their spiritual practice will often hold the letter and return it to you by mail at a specified time.

25

A Few Words on Forgiveness

Prayer Anchor: "So when you are offering your gift
at the altar, if you remember that your brother or sister
has something against you, leave your gift there before
the altar and go; first be reconciled to your brother
or sister, and then come and offer your gift."

Matthew 5:23–24 (NRSV)

This scripture reminds us that our prayers are not as effective when we hold unforgiving thoughts in our minds about ourselves or others. If we truly want our prayers to be felt and experienced, we pray with a receptive mind and heart, free from unresolved issues that block the flow of our good. This scripture tells us to pray with a loving and pure heart. Once our heart is an open channel, the grace of God can flow freely through it, we are changed, and our prayers have added power.

Forgiveness is one of life's most difficult hurdles and yet one of the most important issues we must address to live in health, happiness, and prosperity. When Peter asked Jesus how many times he should forgive, "Jesus said to him, 'Not seven times, but, I tell you, seventy-seven times.'"[1] Seventy-seven times suggests that rather than counting out how many times we forgive, forgiveness is something we'll have to do all of our lives. No matter what the cause of any upset we may experience, we would do well to learn the tools of forgiveness and use them consistently.

If we want to live a God-centered, spiritual, high-quality life, we cannot hang on to hurts from the past. If we want to move forward in love, peace, harmony, and prosperity, we learn to forgive until we make forgiveness a habit and then a way of life. "If someone says, "I love God," and hates his brother, he is a liar; for he who does not love his brother whom he has seen, how can he love God whom he has not seen?"[2]

There are many books written on the subject of forgiveness and how to forgive. The most important thing about forgiving is that we do it. The method is not as important as the fact that we release ourselves from the burden of carrying anger, resentment, guilt, fear, and worry around with us wherever we go. When we suffer over something that has happened in the past, and choose not to do something about it, our own self-love is called into question. Forgiveness is not just a choice we make for ourselves; it is a necessity if we want to enjoy a healthy emotional state of being and lasting relationships with others.

I offer my favorite prayer practice for forgiving because it works. What I have discovered is that the one who truly wants to be free from unforgiving thoughts in his or her mind and heart has already taken a major step toward doing the work of forgiving. I also know that it is important to teach our children at an early age the importance of forgiveness. One of the best ways to teach forgiveness is to model it. Our children will be leagues ahead on their spiritual journey if they see us model forgiveness along with compassion and reconciliation.

Prayer Practice

Read Psalm 51:10. Write in your journal or a notebook your understanding of what this scripture means, especially as it pertains to your ability and willingness to forgive. This will familiarize you with the scripture and begin to impress it in your mind as something that can help you through the forgiveness process.

On a sheet of paper, write the prayer anchor for this chapter (Matthew. 5:23–24) across the top. Below it, make a list of those whom you need to forgive. After each name, briefly state why you want to forgive that person. If you are working with a particular situation, write out your description of the experience briefly and then why you want to forgive everyone related to that experience.

Next, write Psalm 51:10 across the bottom of the page. Say the scripture aloud and then recite the names of those on the list and why you want to forgive them. Each day, for nine consecutive days take a fresh sheet of paper and repeat the process.

After nine days, if you do not feel as though the burden of not being able to forgive has been lifted or at least eased, repeat the process. Remember "seventy-seven times," or as many times as it will take to forgive, is what you want to commit to.

If you are hesitant to forgive a particular person, organization, group of people, etc. on your list, examine your level of willingness to be free of the inner pain that comes with holding onto whatever caused you pain. Do you generally have difficulty letting go of the past? If hanging on to what pains you is what you choose for yourself, you may be in need of some inner work involving self-love.

If you need additional support, here is an affirmation to help with the nine-day forgiveness process. Speak it aloud, write it over and over again in your journal, and spend time meditating on it: *"I love myself enough to let go of what has caused me pain and suffering. I willingly let go of any and all unforgiving thoughts about _____. I prefer to use my energy for productive new opportunities. I am worthy to be free from unloving thoughts so I can move forward using my energy to love me and welcome new possibilities that await me. I love myself enough to make the conscious decision to let go of the past and to move forward with poise, ease, and under grace."*

If, after the nine-day process, you are still having difficulty forgiving and moving on, first be patient with yourself and be persistent in your efforts to forgive. Sometimes the hurt we feel may take some deeper work to clear out. Set aside some time to examine your level of willingness to forgive by journaling what your thoughts and feelings are regarding what you are holding on to. Write out your reasons for holding on to the past. Write until you have exhausted all reasons and excuses for holding on to something that is blocking the flow of good coming into your life. Once you have a feeling of readiness, repeat the prayer practice from the beginning.

If you need to repeat this process, give yourself a two- or three-day break and start fresh with a new nine-day process.

Oftentimes the person we need to forgive is ourselves. If this is the case, perform the above prayer practice using your name. Remember, you deserve to be free of pain and suffering so that you get to enjoy life and the good that you desire.

If you have done this work and still have difficulty with forgiveness, consider getting spiritual counseling or the professional support of a therapist.

26

Money, Money, Money

Prayer Anchor: "And you shall remember the LORD your God, for *it is* He who gives you power to get wealth, …"

Deuteronomy 8:18 (NKJV)

Let's face it. For many of us, there may have been a time when we experienced a temporary cash flow challenge. For some of us, we may find ourselves in this uncomfortable place again at some point. What can we do to prayerfully move through it?

I have often been asked if it is okay to pray for money. My answer is yes. If there is a need, we should indeed pray about it. In fact, if we are vigilant in our prayer life, we pray about everything. We know that, apart from God, we have no financial affairs. If we are attentive to our affairs, we go to God for all our joys and celebrations as well as any concerns or sorrows.

However, it is important to know that whenever we find ourselves in "need," a larger issue is the cause of the lack we are experiencing. In the spiritual law of supply and demand, God has already taken care of the supply side, for in God there can be no lack.

Do you remember in the story of the prodigal son? The older son stayed home, feeling as though he did not have his father's blessing and, more importantly, his father's love? When the younger son, who had squandered his inheritance, returned home, the older son was jealous; he had not claimed his inheritance and erroneously believed he did not have access to it. "And he said to him, 'Son, you are always with me, and all that I have is yours.'"[1]

If we find ourselves believing we do not have access to our full inheritance of supply and every kind of good, let us remember the words the father said to his son: "All that I have is yours." All God's goodness is already ours. If we are not receiving, demonstrating, and enjoying it, then we look at the demand side of the spiritual law of supply and demand. When we are experiencing a cash flow challenge, we need to be clear that money is never the real issue. Unfortunately, money is blamed for far more than that for which it is capable of being responsible. Whenever there is a money issue, you can rest assured that money is innocent.

So, yes, we can pray to receive money as long as we understand and accept that when we experience a short-fall in our cash flow, it is a symptom of a larger challenge related to the demand side of the law. If we pray to have the money we need come to us, we are addressing our situation with a temporary fix. Whatever is behind the appearance of a slowdown in cash flow must eventually be addressed if we do not want to end up in the same situation thirty days later when the bills come due again.

You may already know what the larger challenge is regarding you and money. If not, you can address the demand side of the law by answering some key questions that will help reveal what is at the root of your money issue. This personal inventory will help you to identify where your true prayer work should be directed. Here are a few of the best places to look if cash flow seems to be a recurring challenge:

- What is your overall attitude regarding money, finance, and prosperity?
- Do you pay your bills on time?
- Are you heavily in debt?
- Are you generous in your giving?
- Do you give to spiritual work?

- Are you harboring any anger toward yourself or others?

- Do you manage your financial affairs with integrity, honesty, and wisdom?

- Do you willingly give of your time and talent to help others?

- Do you regularly show your gratitude for the blessings in your life?

- Do you have a personal financial plan with wealth-building strategies in place?

The answers to these kinds of questions will get at the heart of the matter regarding your cash flow situation and will identify where you may look to begin resolving them. Your answers may reveal what has been blocking your ability to draw to you the money you need. Remember, money is never the issue. God is your source, "all that I have is yours," says the spirit of God in you regarding your life and affairs.

There are many books about money management. Make a study of this area if you are having difficulty demonstrating the level of money supply you desire. You will do well to make a study of the spiritual laws regarding money and prosperity as well. For example, the single act of consistently not paying debts on time may be symptomatic of beliefs that have become obstacles to incoming cash flow. From a spiritual perspective, you may need to examine your beliefs about money, the thoughts you hold, and the words you speak regarding money or your lack thereof. In your prayer, you want to get inwardly connected with the divine understanding that God is your source. The prayer anchor reminds us that "God gives us the power to get wealth."

Prayer Practice

In our prayer practice regarding money, we begin by acknowledging God as our source. We let Spirit teach and guide us on what we need to know and do for greater demonstrations in our financial affairs.

Follow this four-step prayer format:

1. Begin your prayer by acknowledging God's presence within you. Let your thoughts be on God as spirit, life, love, and wisdom. Read the prayer anchor of this chapter several times aloud.

2. Fill your mind with thoughts of peace and harmony. It may help to silently affirm, "*I am at peace. I rest in the peaceful presence of God. I am one with the peaceful presence of the Holy Spirit within me.*" Use what has worked for you in the past to get to the state of consciousness where you are not worrying or even thinking about money. Set your mind and heart on a peaceful state of being while acknowledging God's presence.

3. For the purpose of getting at the root of the challenge, ask yourself questions such as the following:

- "*Why am I having trouble with money?*"

- "*What belief am I holding on to that is blocking the flow of money in my life?*"

- "*What must I do to claim the wealth and prosperity that God promises as my divine birthright and true inheritance?*"

- "*What must I change about me to demonstrate greater prosperity in my financial affairs?*"

Ask each question, then sit, wait, and listen inwardly. Do not hurry through this process. Stay open to Spirit and allow the answers to come to you either during your prayer time or in the days ahead.

4. Close your prayer with a time of gratitude. When you genuinely feel a sense of gratitude for your awareness of God's presence, give thanks for the blessings already demonstrated in your life. Thank God for the guidance you have received and will continue to receive regarding your financial affairs.

Your follow-up to the answers you receive will be your new work. As Spirit reveals areas for you to work on, take action or you will again find yourself in a place of cash flow problems.

From a practical standpoint, begin to bless what you already have. Here are a few examples:

- As money comes to you from any and every channel, immediately give thanks for it. Make it a habit of saying, *"Thank you, God, for this money to use and enjoy. I accept it gracefully and use it wisely."*

- When you pay your bills, assume an attitude of gratitude. Give thanks for those creditors who have put their trust in you to pay the bills you have accumulated. Make it important that you operate in integrity with your creditors. Pay them on time. If you are going to be late, call them—don't wait for them to call you. When you pay each bill say, *"Thank you, God, for the money I freely give for the services (or goods) I have received."*

- Practice giving. As soon as you receive money, give ten percent of it to the place where you receive spiritual nourishment. Hold the ten percent you will give in your hands and say, *"I freely give from what I have gratefully received. As I give, I do so with great joy and all that returns to me shall be received in even greater joy and appreciation. Thank you, God!"*

Many churches and spiritual centers have classes, workshops, and seminars to help you expand your consciousness in this area and other areas of your life. Your life and affairs can be changed as you make a commitment to change. Remember money, or the lack thereof, is never the real issue.

27

A Time to Wait

Prayer Anchor: "I waited patiently for the LORD; And
He inclined to me, And heard my cry. He also brought
me up out of a horrible pit, Out of the miry clay, And set
my feet upon a rock, And established my steps. He has
put a new song in my mouth—Praise to our God; Many
will see it and fear, And will trust in the LORD."

Psalm 40:1–3 (NKJV)

In all things, there is a time to wait. For some of us, waiting can be
our most difficult challenge when we have a desire for which we are
praying. In our prayer time, we may feel a strong sense of urgency.
We want our prayers answered immediately. However, the urgent
feeling often grows into anxiety, and anxiety grows to worry, and
worry blocks our receptivity to the answer we've been praying for.

Remember what Jesus had to say about worry? He said, don't
do it! "Therefore I say to you, do not worry about your life..."[1]
Worry can be the mental obstacle that delays our good.

When we make choices based on our own impatience, they often
prove to be less effective and may even be decisions we may later believe
were not the best. Patience can often be the difference between getting
what we desire and getting something that brings difficulties with it.

A waiting prayer is one where we intentionally practice waiting for an answer to be revealed. It may take a few minutes, hours, days, or years. The length of time is not the focus; that we are *willing* to wait for divine guidance is the point. Once we receive an inner response or an outer sign, we will have the strength and power to spring into action. With guidance that comes from the diligent work of patience and giving Spirit time to work on the details to align us with our good, we will feel greater confidence in our steps going forward.

Every prayer we affirm is an idea with its own unique and natural gestation period in our consciousness. The length of the gestation period can range from the second we make the request to many years in the future and everything in between. Our part will be to trust that there is a divine timing for everything. Our prayer or the idea within our prayer may need time to develop into a presence strong enough to travel from the invisible realm to the physical realm. If we can think of our prayers as seeds being planted in the universal pool of ideas, we may be more willing to give them time to take root and grow into healthy manifestations of magnificent demonstrations.

Our prayers may require that the right people and the right set of circumstances be in place before the answer is revealed. Whenever you pray, be willing to give Spirit the time to bring the right circumstances into perfect alignment. When the answer to your prayer does manifest, if you've trusted God enough to wait, you can rest assured that your manifestation is for your highest good, and all who are connected with it will be blessed as well.

Prayer Practice

Begin your time in prayer according to your normal practice, or use any of the prayer practices in this book to which you are drawn. Follow this three-step prayer process:

1. Pray the words from Psalm 40:1–3. Say the words, pray them, feel them, and affirm aloud. Then sit in silence and practice waiting. When we wait in prayer, we are listening inwardly in a relaxed and meditative state. After a time that you feel is sufficient, start the prayer again until you have repeated it three times.

2. After the third recitation, speak your personal prayer request, affirmation, statement, or intention aloud. Then wait on Spirit in silence. In this stage of the process, I suggest you allow yourself at least thirty minutes to an hour of waiting for some shift in your own consciousness. You are waiting for inspiration, guidance, divine ideas, or a revelation of truth from within. Sit in this state of silent waiting for as long as you are guided to do so; this will be when you feel a sense of peace and calmness.

3. Close your time of prayer with a few moments of gratitude. Express your willingness to trust God in the process of waiting.

Stay flexible with the number of days you will use this prayer practice. You may receive an answer the first day, or it may take many days. Either way, know that whatever time you wait in silence, you are preparing for the good you desire. Trust that Spirit has a natural order for things to occur, and your part is to prayerfully wait, knowing the divine right answer or solution will be revealed.

Be aware that a response may come during your prayer time or the course of the minutes and days that follow this process. Stay open to what occurs around you and the thoughts that come to you. Spirit may reveal a response through opportunities that come to you, people you meet, or a set of circumstances made available to you. Stay open and pay attention.

If you journal, this is a great time to write about the thoughts that come to you from praying this prayer. It will help you remain open and allow whatever work needs to occur to be done without anxious, interfering thoughts.

While you are waiting on your answer, don't talk about your prayer request to anyone unless he or she is involved in some way or may be affected by the outcome or unless you are inwardly guided to share with another. If you are truly waiting on the Lord as the prayer anchor says, your need to talk in unnecessary or idle conversation about your prayer may be an indication that you are getting impatient, which is the direct opposite of what this prayer is about. When your response has come, then you may choose to share it with others.

28

The Value of a Spiritual Community

> <u>Prayer Anchor</u>: "Are any among you sick? They should call for the elders of the church and have them pray over them, anointing them with oil in the name of the Lord."
>
> James 5:14–16 (NRSV)

I have often visited hospitals and nursing homes where people had no spiritual community supporting them, praying for them, visiting them, or even remembering them with an occasional card. Not because the community forgot about these people, but because they did not get involved in a spiritual community when they were able to do so.

Too many times I have been asked to officiate at the funeral or memorial service of a person unknown to me and not a member of my spiritual community or another spiritual community. I was certainly happy to assist the family in this situation. However, as the officiator, I must inquire as to who the person was, the kind of life he or she lived, and the contributions made and left as his or her legacy.

Some years ago, a family came to me after their mother had made her transition. The family had been to several churches trying to find someone to officiate their mother's funeral service. They said their mother believed in God but never really attended a church and had no connection with a faith community. One of the three children was involved in a faith community, but this community did not perform services for anyone who was not a member.

The siblings wanted their mother to have what they believed to be a proper burial and came to me frustrated at the rejections they had received. Of course I performed the service. It was a simple service with just a few people attending. None of the family members or friends in attendance spoke during the service. I left the small gathering of people at the cemetery that day wondering why a woman who had lived for more than eighty years seemed to have few connections with family and friends and no extended support system such as a spiritual community. At that point, I could only wonder.

Our prayer anchor illustrates that a spiritual community can be of great value to us. We have a place where we feel comfortable asking for support and giving support. It is important to establish and align ourselves with a support system before we need one. In this way, we grow to higher levels of our spiritual potential when we engage with others through service, giving, receiving, caring, and sharing ourselves with other children of God.

A spiritual community is the place where we expect to find others who have made it their intention to live a life centered in spiritual ideals. Spiritual principles guide and direct us to live out the divine ideals of love, faith, wisdom, peace, harmony, joy, and prosperity. The foundation for everything that is done is centered in these divine ideas. A typical spiritual community will have divine love at the core of the mission, "He said to him, 'You shall love the Lord your God with all your heart, and with all your soul, and with all your mind.' This is the greatest and first commandment. And the second is like it: 'You shall love your neighbor as yourself.'"[1]

When we are an active part of a spiritual community, we have a place where we are accepted and embraced no matter our life circumstances. It is a place of support, friendship, fellowship, and celebration. While each member will grow spiritually at his or her own pace, the collective community will grow to the level of making a difference in the world. We have a loving place where we are reminded of God's love within us and encouraged to express that love on a daily basis.

The greatest benefit, however, is the commitment we make to our own spiritual growth and personal revelation of truth. We make a conscious intention to learn and live the teachings of the spiritual community that we have been drawn to. The gift we receive is an expanded spiritual consciousness and the discovery of our true self. We gain all this for having allowed ourselves to be supported on our journey and giving support to others on theirs.

When we find a spiritual community where we feel safe to be who we are as we grow and are receptive to the teachings of that community, consider being actively involved. Service enhances our overall spiritual growth and provides us with an outlet for our spiritual gifts and talents.

Let the light of God shine forth from you through sharing yourself and supporting others in whatever way you are guided. In this way, you position yourself to receive support at a time when you may need it as well. "In the same way, let your light shine before others, so that they may see your good works and give glory to your Father in heaven."[2]

Prayer Practice

Most spiritual communities have some kind of prayer or chaplain ministry where members are ready to pray one on one with those who ask. If you find yourself desiring prayer support, do not hesitate to ask for it. People who have received the calling to pray with and for others love to do it and will give you their best and highest expression of God's love within them.

Consider getting involved in a group that prays for others. Your own prayer life will be enhanced as you pray with and for others. If praying with others is not your calling, find some area where you may volunteer in your chosen spiritual community. I have discovered that those who are actively involved enjoy a deeper spiritual experience in their own personal lives and with others in the community.

You don't have to be a formal member of a prayer ministry to pray for the members of your spiritual community. Make this part of your regular prayer practice. Pray for all who serve in spiritual leadership roles. The stronger and more prayed up they are, the more they can give to the community as a whole. You want them to know that they are surrounded by others who see them expressing God's life, love, and wisdom in all they do. With the prayers of others, they will continue to be blessed in their own lives. When their personal affairs are harmonious, it will affect their ability and desire to effectively serve the community as a whole.

Pray for the members of your faith community that all may live and express the presence and power of God individually and as a collective body. See your spiritual community being an example of peace on earth.

In your time of prayer, visualize your whole community of faith bathed in a white light of God's presence. See the individual members centered in peaceful harmony with each other while serving and living God's will for their life. Affirm that the entire community demonstrates the purpose attributed to the organization's mission as a whole. "For just as the body is one and has many members, and all the members of the body, though many, are one body, so it is with Christ."[3]

Finally, I have seen solid friendships develop between people as a result of being involved within a spiritual community, and a few marriages also. With its many opportunities to meet and interact with like-minded people, an active spiritual community can be a great blessing and a strong support system for navigating life's journey.

29

Praying the Psalms

Prayer Anchor: "Where can I go from your spirit?
Or where can I flee from your presence? If I ascend to
heaven, you are there; if I make my bed in Sheol, you are
there. If I take the wings of the morning and settle at
the farthest limits of the sea, even there your hand shall
lead me, and your right hand shall hold me fast."

Psalm 139:7–10 (NRSV)

The book of Psalms is one of the most popular books in the Bible. The Psalms are a collection of poems, hymns, and prayers. The prayer anchor for this chapter gives a good overall theme for the book of Psalms—a timeless lesson that we all want and need to know: we can never be separated from God.

Psalm 139 confirms that no matter where we go or what we do, we are never out of reach of the hand of God. We discover that we can count on God to be there for us even when we are not living up to the best of who and what we are. The message is, wherever we are, God's loving presence is there as well. The hand of God is steady. It holds us through the falls we sustain and softens the hurt, lifts us up from the errors we make, guides us through times of change, and nurtures and nourishes us as we grow. But no matter what, the hand of God is always on us.

In the Psalms, we find writings that confirm over and over that God's presence is always with us. We see it expressed as strength, trust, praise, thanksgiving, celebration, and compassion between God and the writers of this inspirational collection of work. We feel a deep connection and empathy with the authors of the various psalms as we read them. Whenever we witness God's compassionate attention to the prayers of others, we are moved by it and desire the same for ourselves. The psalmists lived in hope, and we get a glimpse of that hope for ourselves as we read through the powerful words of devotion, love, and humility toward God.

Because the Psalms have been prayed and sung for thousands of years, their vibrant energy cannot help but be one of faith, strength, and power. The person who prays them with the spiritual discernment of an evolving consciousness will experience results beyond measure.

It is important to get into the feeling of the words and not stuck in the literal wording of some of the psalms. The authors wrote from their own experience and the consciousness through which they lived at the time. You and I can pray these same Psalms, the same words, and apply an expanded consciousness that is relevant to our spiritual understanding.

For example, in some of the psalms, you will read of the anger and desire for vengeance on the part of the person who is praying. Read the words, understanding that the writer wants to portray deep feelings of pain and the level of suffering that only God can heal. If you have ever had moments of deep anger, you may remember that your thoughts may not have been very loving in that moment. So be gentle with the psalmist as his pain was deep, and he trusted enough to pour them out to the one whom he knew could address them properly: God.

As you read the words, know that it takes great strength and trust in God to be open and honest about whatever you are feeling. Your goal is to attain that level of openness and honesty in your unfolding relationship with God. In this light, you will pray with the same knowing that the psalmists did. God can heal any and every erroneous thought, belief, and action we have created in our consciousness. So lay them out for God to heal rather than ignore them and be forever bound to them.

In reading the words of the Psalms, allow the movement of spirit within you to heal, lift, bless, and prosper whatever situation you are growing through. The psalmists prayed from where they were in consciousness, and this precipitated the spiritual growth that allowed them to discover, "The Lord is my shepherd, I shall not want."[1] "For it was you who formed my inward parts; you knit me together in my mother's womb. I praise you, for I am fearfully and wonderfully made."[2] "The Lord is my light and my salvation; whom shall I fear?"[3] "Great is the Lord, and greatly to be praised; his greatness is unsearchable."[4] The testimonies of the psalmists go on and on.

Here are a few of my favorite Psalms and some of the themes connected with each one:

Psalm 23: Pray this Psalm when your prayer desire is for protection or healing of any kind; to address financial concerns; to cure thoughts of lack and limitation; to reduce feelings of fear or worry; to stimulate inner peace, divine guidance, comfort, and gratitude; or for a loved one who has made his or her transition.

Psalm 91: Pray this Psalm when you desire to reconfirm God's protection or control anxious and fearful thoughts when you are facing difficulties. Verses 14–16 are God's response to the love, loyalty, and trust the Psalmist demonstrates toward God. Specifically pray this part when you feel the need to know God's love, protection, and blessings are on your life.

Psalm 112: Pray this prayer when you desire to put God first in your life, success and prosperity for a new endeavor, guidance in business affairs, protection in business transactions, or to develop a consciousness of charitable giving.

Psalm 119: This Psalm is the quintessential prayer/meditation for attaining divine guidance. Also pray this Psalm to strengthen your faith and develop discipline in spiritual matters.

Psalm 121: Pray this prayer for safety in traveling for yourself or loved ones.

Psalm 139: This is a great Psalm to pray and meditate on when you feel lost, alone, separated from God, fearful, in need of divine guidance, unworthy, low in self-esteem or self-consciousness, unloved, or need assurance that your loved ones are in God's care and keeping. This is also the reassurance of God's love and constant presence.

Psalm 150: This prayer celebrates God at work in our lives. Pray this as a prayer of gratitude and thanksgiving.

Prayer Practice

I suggest first reading through the entire book of Psalms and making a personal list of those that speak to you. Use your list from which to make your selections when you choose to use this particular prayer practice.

Select one of the Psalms that speaks to you and addresses your particular prayer desire. Read through the entire Psalm to understand the theme, and choose the verse(s) that particularly speaks to your prayer request.

Use your own guidance and intuition as to how the scripture verse(s) may best be used; however, here is a general format:

- Set your intention on the number of days to pray the prayer you have selected (three, seven, nine, twenty-one, or forty).

- In your journal, prayerfully write the verse(s) you will use three times each morning followed by your specific prayer request.

- Each evening, just before going to sleep, prayerfully read your selected verse(s) aloud nine times from your Bible, meditating on the words and their meaning. Do not revisit your specific prayer request for the evening session.

- During the length of this prayer practice, stay open to ideas and opportunities that are sure to present themselves. Stay open and prepare to take action on any guidance received.

Another method of praying the powerful Psalms is to focus on the scripture you select verse by verse. Take one verse per day until you have prayed, meditated, and journaled on the entire Psalm. Take one final day to meditate on the entire Psalm. Ask in prayer for the meaning the verses of this Psalm have for your life and their value to your prayer desire. Journaling through this process can be enlightening and empowering. The key is to pray the Psalm that addresses your own particular purpose for prayer.

For example, Psalm 119 may be prayed verse by verse or section by section particularly since it is the longest of the Psalms. It would take 177 days to complete, one verse per day with one day for the final review of the total scripture. If you wanted to make a prayer of this in a shorter time, you could divide it up into sections and take one section each day with one day for the final overview.

Praying the Psalms is well worth the time in prayerful study and meditation for it will deepen your faith and understanding of God's divine law and grace.

Part 5

Prayer Practices for
a Deeper Spiritual
Experience

30

Fast and Pray

<u>Prayer Anchor:</u> "Go, gather all the Jews to be found
in Susa, and hold a fast on my behalf, and neither eat nor
drink for three days, night or day. I and my maids will also
fast as you do. After that I will go to the king, though it is
against the law; and if I perish, I perish. ... On the third day
Esther put on her royal robes and stood in the inner court of
the king's palace. ... As soon as the king saw Queen Esther
standing in the court, she won his favor and he held out to
her the golden scepter that was in his hand. ... The king
said to her, 'What is it, Queen Esther? What is your request?
It shall be given you, even to the half of my kingdom.'"

Esther 4:16; 5:1–3 (NRSV)

The book of Esther has long been one of my favorite stories. It
has intrigue, romance, mystery, divine intervention, and a happy
ending—many of the qualities we enjoy seeing on a big screen at
the movies.

As the story is told, after Esther became Queen, the life of
her people was threatened. Esther found herself in the position of
spiritual leadership, and she rose to the occasion in grand style. We
don't know what Esther's prayer life was like before she called a

three-day fast and prayer vigil, but we do know that she was raised by her cousin Mordecai who was a devout Jew. Esther knew that this was the thing to do.

She asked the Jews to fast on her behalf and neither eat nor drink for three days, night or day. She said she would be fasting as well. After three days, she would ask the king to spare their lives, knowing she would be putting herself in danger by doing so.

What you may or may not know is that after the book of Esther had been translated from Hebrew into Greek, six additions totaling 107 verses were added to Esther's story. They are recorded in what is called the Apocrypha. There, the story is told a little differently in that Esther does not call a fast, but she does hold her own three-day prayer vigil.

Queen Esther changes her clothing from her royal attire and puts on "garments of distress and mourning … she utterly humbled her body, and every part that she loved to adorn she covered with her tangled hair."[1] She prayed for three days, and on the third day, when she ended her prayer, "She took off the garments in which she had worshiped, and arrayed herself in splendid attire."[2] Esther goes before the king, putting her own life in danger by doing so. The king not only listens to her but also gives her what she asks for. The lives of her people are spared, and justice is brought about for the culprit who attempted to have the Jews killed in the first place.

What a story! One version speaks to fasting and the other to praying. They are both correct. The ancients often accompanied prayer with their time of fasting. These two powerful spiritual practices together make for the movement of spirit on our prayers in a powerful way. A fast is a set period of time we take to do inner cleansing and deep spiritual work. We fast by abstaining from negativity and erroneous thinking as mental and spiritual cleansing work; we fast for inner physical cleansing by abstaining from solid food and, in some cases, liquid as well. Combined, fasting for mental, spiritual, and physical cleansing forms a ripe consciousness for grand new possibilities.

In ancient times and under religious practice, fasting was thought to be a humbling experience that demonstrated the faith and discipline necessary to prepare for approaching God with specific requests. In the scriptures, where there was fasting and praying, God found favor on those who prayed; they felt and believed their prayers were answered because they humbled themselves by fasting and because they approached God with reverence through focused prayer. "So we fasted and entreated our God for this, and He answered our prayer."[3] People fasted and prayed because they got results.

As a spiritual practice, fasting has two levels. The first level occurs when we do a mental cleansing. We fast from negative thoughts and feelings. This clears the mind and prepares us mentally to receive the wisdom of Spirit from within. The second level involves fasting from solid food for a physical cleansing. At this level, we gather the support of the physical body to aid a more complete cleansing process. When the bodily functions involved in the digestive process are free to relax, that unused energy is directed to support the mental focus toward purifying our thoughts.

Fasting and praying brings together the physical, mental, emotional, and spiritual aspects of our being. In this way, we give our prayer request the full support of all that we are. We set ourselves apart from our normal routines and declare this prayer request a high priority in our lives; therefore, the answer becomes a high priority for the power of God within us.

If you choose to incorporate fasting from solid food into your spiritual practice, it is important that you do not do so without the advice of your health care professional. If you have certain ailments and health conditions, fasting from solid food can cause more harm than good to your body. So please get professional help before you attempt a fast. I can share with you only my experience with the hope that it helps you develop this spiritual practice, along with the appropriate assistance of your health care professional.

I have fasted for one, three, seven, nine, and twenty-one days on varying occasions for different purposes. What works for me now is one or three days. When I did an extended fast, it was with specific mental, physical, and spiritual goals that were prayerfully directed. I fasted from solid food (outer) and negative thoughts by way of focused prayer (inner).

I would not do an extended fast (anything over seven days) without some kind of support system or medical advice. When I did my twenty-one-day fast, I did so with a group of like-minded friends. We supported each other and served as a watchful eye, assuring that we were each disciplined but remained healthy and focused.

I do, however, admire the Islamic annual spiritual practice of prayer and fasting for a month of Ramadan. Muslims fast from all food and drink from sunup to sundown for thirty days of focused prayer. The breaking of the fast at sundown is often a time for celebration with family and community while sharing a delicious meal. The support of the entire religious community during this annual time of prayer and fasting lends itself to a deep spiritual experience.

I have tried the sunup to sundown prayer and fasting with Muslim friends and found it difficult to do for the entire month. So while I admire this practice of my Muslim brothers and sisters, it is not my particular choice for this type of spiritual practice. When I fast, I ingest no solid food for the prescribed time, taking in only fresh juices and lots of water. These days, I use fresh, organic vegetables for juicing and, to a limited extent, I'll juice some fruit. Although I am aware that all-water fasts are successful for some, it is not my personal preference having discovered it to be too hard on my body for more than a day. A water-only fast should be done under medical supervision and with great spiritual clarity on the purpose of such a fast.

After about three days of fasting and praying, my experience has been that my dreams are more vivid and my meditations are deeper. I feel more at peace, and do not require as much sleep. Whenever I have incorporated fasting from solid food with my prayers, I have incorporated journaling. I keep notes on the experience, paying careful attention to the mental, emotional, spiritual, and physical changes in me during the process. I have always been blessed with many benefits when combining fasting with my prayers.

I would suggest you read up on fasting before doing one. Lots of books have been written on the subject. Do your homework if you are serious about fasting. I'm not attempting to give health advice here; however, there are many other healthful suggestions to complement your fasting that you will want to know about. For example, most books that speak of fasting will tell you to eat easily digestible foods in the days prior to and after your fast—no dairy, no meat, no animal fat. You need to know this kind of information if you want fasting and praying to be a successful experience.

I have discovered that my body enjoys a good fast from solid food from time to time. When I fast, I have increased energy and mental and spiritual clarity. Quite frankly, when I fast from solid food and negative thoughts together, I feel great.

If you are not in a situation where you may fast from solid food or choose not to do it, you may fast from negative thinking, and this is always an effective use of the practice of fasting.

When we humble ourselves, as we do by fasting and praying, we are doing our inner work that sets the stage for answered prayer. In this way, we condition our mind with faith and great expectancy.

Prayer Practice

Get specific on your prayer desire and the purpose for adding fasting to your prayer.

- Put your prayer in writing.

- Decide on the length of your fast (one, three, seven, nine, twenty-one, or forty days). I've never done a prayer/fast for longer than twenty-one days. However, in the Gospels, it is mentioned that Jesus fasted and prayed for forty days. I would be careful in deciding on a forty-day fast and would not do it unless under medical guidance.

- Gather the items you will need for your fast. It is important to have what you need at hand for your fast. It will help you to stay focused and disciplined toward your goal.

- Set your fast in motion, and begin your prayer. Pray your prayer at least three times each day of your fast. You'll discover a greater value in your fasting with more time spent in prayer; one full hour in prayer each of the three times you pray will yield positive benefits. Your prayers have added power when you give yourself time to sit in silent prayer or quiet contemplation of truth with your request.

Remember, you are fasting from negative thoughts as well as solid food. You will want to limit watching TV, reading newspapers, and listening to the radio, as these media are where we pick up so much negativity, many times without even realizing it.

When you pray and fast for a specific purpose, it is also a good time to bring in some of the other prayer practices mentions in this book, such as lighting candles, burning incense, or taking a spiritual bath. Plan to enjoy the experience; you'll gain even greater blessings if you do.

31

Know Your Spiritual Gifts

<u>Prayer Anchor:</u> "At Gibeon the Lord appeared to Solomon in a dream by night; and God said, 'Ask what I should give you.' 'Give your servant therefore an understanding mind to govern your people, able to discern between good and evil; for who can govern this your great people?' It pleased the Lord that Solomon had asked this. God said to him, 'Because you have asked this, and have not asked for yourself long life or riches, or for the life of your enemies, ... I now do according to your word. Indeed I give you a wise and discerning mind; ... I give you also what you have not asked, both riches and honor all your life; ...'"

1 Kings 3:5, 9–13 (NRSV)

As a child in Sunday school, I heard my teachers talk of the wisdom of Solomon. In the church where I grew up, we often talked about Bible characters, but for some reason, Solomon was one who intrigued me most. I wanted to know how Solomon got to be so wise. What made him so special that God blessed him with such wisdom that he would be admired and talked about thousands of years after he was gone?

Not until I was an adult did I read 1 Kings 3. I learned that Solomon was a praying man who loved God and wanted to serve God with his whole heart. "Solomon loved the Lord, walking in the statutes of his father David."[1] He received wisdom from God because he was open to it and asked for it. That's it. Solomon wanted to live up to the mighty responsibility placed on him. His desire was so strong that when God came to him in a dream and asked him what he wanted, his response was—wisdom, an understanding heart!

The added bonus in the story is that God heard Solomon's request and was pleased that Solomon had not asked for something that would suggest selfish gain. Solomon desired wisdom not for himself but to serve God and the people of Israel. For his humility, God granted Solomon with both riches and honor to be enjoyed for the rest of his life. Solomon is thought to be the wisest man in the Old Testament, but he is also thought to be the wealthiest in the entire Bible.

Wisdom is one of many spiritual gifts identified in the New Testament. It is one of many gifts that God has made available to us when we choose to serve God by helping others. We all have spiritual gifts. They show up in our lives as those things that we have a natural interest and talent for—skills that fit well with our purpose in life. Solomon was chosen as heir to the throne, succeeding his father. David had been a beloved king, and under his leadership Israel grew and prospered. So Solomon knew he would need wisdom to follow the awesome leadership standard set by his father before him. Wisdom was what he needed to serve God to the highest of his ability, and God granted it and so much more.

Whatever we are called to do or for whatever our purpose, our Creator wants us to have what we need to fulfill the task. You can recognize your spiritual gifts by the things that you like to do and the things that you have a natural talent for. These are the kinds of things people ask you to do for them or help them do. These are the kinds of talents you willingly share to serve God and help others.

"To each is given the manifestation of the spirit for the common good. To one is given through the spirit the utterance of wisdom, and to another the utterance of knowledge according to the same Spirit, to another faith by the same Spirit, to another gifts of healing by the one Spirit, to another the working of miracles, to another prophecy, to another the discernment of spirits, to another various kinds of tongues, to another the interpretation of tongues. All these are activated by one and the same Spirit, who allots to each one individually just as the Spirit chooses."[2]

In this scripture, we see many spiritual gifts identified. When these gifts are used for the common good or to help others, they are spiritual gifts. References to other spiritual gifts can be found by being open to them as you read through the scriptures.

"We have gifts that differ according to the grace given to us: prophecy, in proportion to faith; ministry, in ministering; the teacher, in teaching; the exhorter, in exhortation, the giver, in generosity; the leader in diligence; the compassionate, in cheerfulness."[3]

There are a variety of gifts to be used in service to God and many opportunities to share them. Each person is to use his or her God-given gifts for the nourishment and uplifting of others in unselfish service. God has given us spiritual gifts that we may access to help, serve, and care for others. If we sincerely desire to use those gifts, we will be guided to opportunities where we may share them.

Like Solomon, we can ask from within to receive the gifts we need to be and do what God has guided us to do. When we say yes to God's plan for our lives, we invite the opportunity to be strengthened in those areas that will allow us to serve to our highest ability.

Solomon was blessed with riches and honor for the humility he expressed in his sincere desire to follow the divine path laid out before him to be king of Israel. Solomon knew he could not thrive in the awesome tasks before him from his ego or personality; he needed and wanted the wisdom of God. He demonstrated his true greatness when he asked God to provide what he needed to follow his divine path. He asked, and God responded with more than Solomon ever even imagined—riches and honor.

Prayer Practice

This is the prayer practice of an unselfish heart. The purpose is to have Spirit reveal from within the gifts that are especially yours to be used to honor God and be of service in the world.

Write each of these fifteen spiritual gifts on an index card along with a short definition (one per card). I give a brief definition here, however you may want to do some further study and write your understanding of the gift on the card as well: wisdom, as inner knowing; knowledge as the ability to gather and retain intellectual information; faith as having a strong belief in God; healing, as the ability to see wholeness regardless of appearances; working of miracles, as the ability to work with spiritual laws from a high point of view; prophecy, the ability to receive divine inspiration and share with others; discernment, the ability to understand matters without knowing all the facts; speaking in tongues, the ability to communicate prayer and praise in unknown languages or through creative expression; interpretation of tongues, the ability to put in plain words prayers given in an unknown language; ministering, a divine calling to support others in their spiritual growth; teaching, the ability to communicate knowledge effectively; exhortation, the ability to encourage and comfort others; generosity, to give of resources freely and liberally; leadership, the ability to guide others in a particular direction; compassion, the ability to feel deep empathy for others and act toward them with kindness.

- In your time of prayer, read 1 Corinthians 12.

- Take one index card per day to meditate on. Hold the card in your hand, and when you are in a relaxed and prayerful state, focus your attention inwardly and say something to this effect: *"God within me fills my desire to be of service. I am divinely guided now."* Repeat this several times.

- Spend the remainder of your time in prayer, meditating on the word on the index card. Repeat the word several times. Do not try to force an inner response; you want a natural, spirit-guided revelation of the gifts that are yours to be used in service.

- Close this time with a prayer of gratitude for the inner guidance to discover your spiritual gifts.

- Carry the card with you throughout the day. Look at it occasionally during the day as a reminder that you are seeking an inner response from Spirit concerning that particular spiritual gift. Are there any opportunities to express that gift during the day? During this time especially, notice any messages you may receive from others. Notice the situations you find yourself in, always with an open mind to discover the spiritual gifts you could bring to the experience. Spirit reveals answers in a variety of ways, so stay open and in tune with your desire to discover your spiritual gifts.

- At the end of the day, write on the back of the card any responses and reactions you received regarding the gift you were working with for the day.

- Repeat this process, using one card per day until all the index cards have been included in your prayer.

Since fifteen gifts are listed, this process will take fifteen days to complete. Go through the same process with each gift. From some gifts, you may receive a strong sense that you have this gift, but for others, you may have a lesser reaction. During this process, journaling will be helpful. Write out the experiences that you have and what comes to you during meditations. Take time to assess what you have received in prayer and what you discerned overall regarding this process. The key is to stay open.

After you have completed the fifteen day process, you should be able to narrow your list down to about three to six gifts. These gifts will be those that you have some inner leaning toward or interest in developing. Take those gifts to three or four people who are close to you and know you well. Ask them if they think you have any of these qualities already, and if so, to prioritize them in the order they feel you exhibit them. This will narrow your list down to about three to four gifts, and these will become your short list to focus on in your prayer time. Don't skip this step. Oftentimes those close to us can see in us what we cannot see in ourselves. When two of your three people agree on the priority of the same gift, you can feel safe to include it as one of your gifts.

In your next available prayer time, focus on one gift at a time from your short list. Affirm, *"I am grateful for the spiritual gift of _____ so that I may be of maximum service to God and those around me. I am open to using this gift as I am divinely guided and directed for the good of all concerned. Thank you, God."*

If you do this process prayerfully, you will be guided to the spiritual gifts you are to share with others and a place to joyfully express those gifts through service. Share your spiritual gifts lovingly and generously, and you will find great personal fulfillment

By engaging in this prayer practice, you will open yourself up to new opportunities to share your spiritual gifts through service. In your daily life, stay open to opportunities where you may be invited or interested in volunteering your gifts. Although service is its own reward, you can expect to receive from others the same quality of generosity with which you give. The confirmation of your spiritual gifts will be the manner in which you share them and the personal fulfillment and enjoyment you experience in the process.

Do this exercise again after about six months of using the spiritual gifts you identified. This will help confirm the gift and may identify other gifts that you are developing in the process.

32

Chanting

Prayer Anchor: "When you are praying, do not heap up empty phrases as the Gentiles do; for they think that they will be heard because of their many words. Do not be like them, for your Father knows what you need before you ask him."

Matthew 6:7–8 (NRSV)

Chanting has a long history in religious and spiritual practices. Chanting can be described as a word or a phrase that is repeated in rhythmic form with or without music. What determines whether chanting is a religious or spiritual practice are the words or phrases used, the intention behind it, and the desire to gain what focused repetition can do for the mind, heart, body, and soul.

When picketers march around a building repeating over and over their statements of complaint, this is also chanting. While it is chanting, it does not come under the heading of religious and spiritual practices. When the words or phrases we speak in rhythmic repetition are godly ideas or ideas related to expressing and expanding our spirituality, this is chanting as part of a prayer practice.

Reading the prayer anchor for this chapter, someone could erroneously interpret that Jesus is against the repetition of words when we pray, but Jesus' statement is more concerned with empty phrases being repeated under the guise of praying. Empty phrases are words that have no foundation in truth. They are not positive or uplifting in quality and character. They are worry statements, begging and pleading toward an unwilling God.

Jesus makes the point that our prayers should not be empty words but rather words and phrases of truth and divine love. The words that we would speak in repetition should be words that uplift, inspire, bless, heal, and prosper. Our repetitions should acknowledge God's presence and power within us and in the world.

We don't speak "many words" with the intention to contact God or to get God to hear our prayers. This is not the purpose behind chanting for spiritual purposes. Our prayers are always intended to change us, not God. Repetition allows us the opportunity to anchor in our conscious and subconscious the realization that God is always present and available to us. We repeat empowering phrases so that we can align ourselves with the grace and power of God within.

Once we experience the deep communion with God that is possible through chanting, we realize God has heard us from the first word. We've simply activated our desire. We come to know firsthand that God already knows what we need before we ask. In the case of chanting, we need to feel God's presence even if we call it something else. We chant to have a conscious experience with God, to be fully aware of our oneness with our Creator and all of creation. This is what chanting for spiritual and religious practice can do for the one who sincerely wants to experience God's presence through prayer.

Chanting prepares us to hear the still, small voice of God within. A simple chant turns into a meeting with God, a divine appointment with our Creator. We may have thought we had an agenda before meeting God in prayer, but we soon discover the experience itself is really a gift and the opportunity to be still and know God.

Prayer Practice

In Western religions, chanting generally isn't part of spiritual practice to the same degree as our brothers and sisters in the East. So in your own spiritual community, you may not experience chanting on a regular basis. Even so, there are many recordings that can help you if chanting is of interest to you. And yes, you can have a deep and profound experience by using a CD or a DVD session as your guide to learn the process.

It may take some trial and error to determine the chant that speaks to you, but it will be worth it if you are serious about adding this to your spiritual practice. The important thing is to be patient. If you use a CD, for example, learn the chants so that you may speak them along with the recording until you can do the chants on your own.

You may even want to form a group in your spiritual community who will join together and chant as a prayerful experience. Great value can be gained when each member shares his or her individual experiences.

Also, make up your own phrases to chant. Whatever you desire to experience, chant it until its harmonic expression feels like a song or a melodic flow. Say it over and over again, and a rhythm will emerge. Stay with it and let it unfold for you.

Some years ago, I wanted to feel God as love in me. I began affirming over and over again, "God is love, God loves me." I said it hundreds of times during the day and finally began to take the words in prayer. As I inhaled, I would say, "God is love"; as I exhaled, I would say, "God loves me." Focusing on breathing helped form a rhythm that soon took me deeper into myself until I reached a place within where I knew the words that I was saying were true. Without realizing it, a tune emerged and I was chanting, "God is love, God loves me" as though it were a song coming from my soul.

Just remember Jesus' warning: do not heap up empty phrases, but consciously speak with focused repetition words of truth, wisdom, love, and power, and chanting will be a great blessing to your spiritual experience.

33

Breathe

<u>Prayer Anchor</u>: "The Spirit of God has made me, and the breath of the Almighty gives me life."

Job 33:4 (NKJV)

There is a wonderful movie titled *Ever After*, a love story that I enjoy watching. There is a scene in the movie where the character played by Drew Barrymore is about to make a grand entrance to meet the man she has fallen in love with. He does not know her true identity, and this is the night she must tell him that she is not a countess but a servant. She is dressed like a fairy princess, and on entering the ball where he is waiting for her, with many guests looking on, she stands tall and says to herself, "Breathe."

Did you ever have one of those moments? A "just breathe" moment? When we are stressed, upset, angry, or even overly excited, it seems we don't breathe as we should. Our breathing is shallow and cut off. In moments like these, we remind ourselves to breathe.

When I gave birth to my children, and probably when I was born, the attending physician would first tap the baby on the bottom to help him or her catch that first breath, and the body would render its first sound. It was to get the lungs working and help the baby open the throat area and start breathing. I remember the doctor saying to me that it is good for a newborn baby to cry. (Apparently, it exercises their lungs, and strong lungs make for good, natural, healthy breathing).

There are healthy and unhealthy ways to breathe. Shallow breathing cuts off a good flow of oxygen which the body needs for healthy functioning. The body consistently without the oxygen it receives through deep, full breathing can cause stress to the body and mind. Poor breathing habits can contribute to illness. Unfortunately, unless we take a class on the importance of, or that teaches the techniques of healthy breathing, the only training we get concerning proper breathing is that first tap on the bottom that the doctor gave us on the day of our birth.

As part of our spiritual practices, healthy breathing can help facilitate clearing the mind and opening the way to a deeper prayer experience. There are workshops, books, and tapes to guide the process of consciously focusing on breathing. But for our purpose and this prayer practice, to breathe deeply and fully will help move you to the place of inner quietude that will enhance your prayer experience.

Prayer Practice

One way to incorporate conscious breathing into your prayer time is to do the following:

- Sit upright in a straight-backed chair with both feet flat on the floor, hands resting on your lap.

- Focus on your breathing. Pay attention to the rise and fall of your chest. Breathe deeply and slowly. Inhale through your nose; exhale slowly through your mouth. Practice breathing like this until you fall into a rhythm. This should take you to a relaxed state.

- Reflect on the scripture from Job: "The Spirit of God has made me, and the breath of the Almighty gives me life."[1] Relax even more as you think the word "relax" and continue to breathe deeply and fully. On the inhalation, silently affirm, "*The spirit of God has made me,* and on the exhalation, silently affirm, *and the breath of the Almighty gives me life.*"

- When you are ready to conclude your prayer, fill your mind with thoughts of peace and harmony. If there is some prayer desire that you have, without addressing it, express gratitude for the right outcome of whatever the situation.

- Continue to breathe and relax, open your eyes slowly, and remain in this peaceful state for as long as you can.

Go about your business for the day with a refreshed spirit. Whenever you remember throughout the day, take a moment to relax and just consciously breathe. As you practice this more and more, you will notice that even one minute in the middle of a busy day can provide a sense of peace if you consciously take time to breathe.

34

Pray for a Vision

<u>Prayer Anchor</u>: "Then the Lord answered me and said: Write the vision; make it plain on tablets, so that a runner may read it. For there is still a vision for the appointed time; it speaks of the end and does not lie. If it seems to tarry, wait for it; it will surely come, it will not delay."

Habakkuk. 2:2–3 (NRSV)

I have been consciously setting goals for myself for at least the last twenty-five years. For many years, I used a journal to record my goals. Goal setting has made a difference in my life and helped me continually craft a vision toward which to direct my life. Having a goal announces where I want to go; having a vision says I can see myself getting there. And if we are in the midst of crafting a vision that is compelling, life can feel exciting even when things aren't going as we hope they would.

The book of Proverbs is considered to be biblical teachings on wisdom. It is filled with instructions and guidance on how to lead and live life by making wise decisions and choices. One of those kernels of wisdom is "Where there is no vision, the people perish,"[1] also put as "Where there is no prophecy, the people cast off restraint."[2]

No matter which version you choose to follow, both reveal an important lesson: it is wise to have a personal vision. Without a vision, we flounder from project to project, job to job, relationship to relationship, etc. We are not clear on where we are going, nor do we know where we want to go. Someone once said, "If you don't know where you're going, any road will take you there." Without some sense of where we're going or where we'd like to go, our day-to-day, week-to-week, month-to-month, and year-to-year activities are just that—activities. Consider the cat that chases its tail: There's lots of activity, but the cat really doesn't go anywhere. Activity does not equal progress toward crafting the life you desire.

For most of my early work life, I was what I called a job-hopper. I started working when I was sixteen and right out of high school. I would work at a job for about two years, and then a feeling of discontent would stir in me and I had to move on. I would get bored and create some reason why I had to leave. Even after I finished college, I would spend two years on a job and then I was seeking somewhere else to go. Finally, I thought starting my own business to share my talents would get me settled into one place. Well, four years and two businesses later, I had a spiritual experience that guided me into ministry.

After two years as the spiritual leader of a center in Miami, I started to feel uneasy, knowing my history. I wondered if I would create some grand reason to leave. But the real opportunity came after the third year. I was faced with a good reason to leave: a few people wanted me to and made it well known. For a time I thought, "This is it. My past has caught up with me once again." I began mentally preparing to leave.

But what I had not counted on was a flashback of the vision I had been given. When I took my ordination for ministry, I was given a vision of serving in a vibrant, spirit-filled ministry. So there I was, three years in Miami with the opportunity to leave. I was face to face with a defining moment to either go or stay—to fill my present with more of my past or a chance to embrace a new reality for myself.

I remember the night before the congregational meeting, I sat in prayer and said something like, "Dear God, lead me to the vibrant, spirit-filled ministry where I am to serve." After sitting in silence with this request on my heart for what seemed to be all of two minutes, an inner response came to me: "You are already there. Stay." I did.

The turning point for me was personally realizing the power of vision for my life. Once there is a vision, it helps to make the major and minor decisions we will be faced with in life. The vision becomes the litmus test by which we gauge and measure our choices.

Our vision may involve being the best we can be in our relationships with others, making a meaningful contribution to society through our careers, living a healthy lifestyle, expressing personal spiritual growth as an example for others, living a life of generosity, or whatever speaks to our hearts and souls. When we open ourselves to a personal vision from God, our receptivity is like a magnet that draws to us new possibilities—and we are drawn where we need to be, to do what is ours to do.

In the book of Habakkuk, we are given key ingredients on receiving a vision from God. We must be willing to prayerfully wait for a vision from within. The vision we want is a God-directed one. We want the guidance, clarity, and blessings of harmony and prosperity to unfold in our lives with ease and under grace. So we wait. If the vision seems to be delayed, we wait in prayer, meditation, and silence, knowing it will surely come. Habakkuk tells us to write it down. When we write what has been revealed, we bring clarity of thought to the vision we receive.

I often hear people talk about wanting to know their purpose. Purpose comes with a prayerfully discerned vision. In prayer, we set our intention to be open to God's plan for our lives. When we prayerfully open ourselves to greater possibilities for our lives, God's vision will surely come, and our purpose is revealed.

The process is threefold: first, accept that there is a divine plan for your life; second, be open to letting it be revealed; and third, cooperate with the unfolding guidance as it begins to manifest.

First, let's consider how we know there is a divine plan. I like the scripture that tells of Jeremiah's call: "Now the word of the Lord came to me saying, 'Before I formed you in the womb I knew you, and before you were born I consecrated you; I appointed you a prophet to the nations.'"[3]

It was revealed to Jeremiah that his life is important, meaningful, and backed by a divine plan with a specific purpose. Before he was born, God had an idea that Jeremiah was brought forth to fulfill. This became the vision for his life. It was God given and God driven.

The same is true for you and me. Each of us has been brought forth with an important and meaningful life, backed by a divine plan with a specific purpose that may be achieved through a variety of ways. We pray to gain access to the divine plan that is uniquely ours and to embrace the opportunities that unfold in a purposeful life.

The second part of the process is being open. When it was first revealed to me that spiritual leadership was my purpose, I did not accept it. I was not open to it. It meant changes in my life that I thought I had to make on my own, and they seemed far beyond my reach and understanding at that time. I was resistant until many outer signs were revealed. The words from Habakkuk present great advice, "If it seems to tarry, wait for it." The scripture warns us that sometimes we must be patient as the vision is revealed to us. The vision may seem delayed, or we are not quite ready to embrace it. Either way, if we will stay committed to the prayer and follow divine guidance, the vision will surely be revealed, and we will be ready to receive it at the right time.

Third, cooperation is required on our part. So often we do not cooperate with God's good that has already been laid out before us. We may even indulge in self-sabotage and become the roadblock to our own prayers. "And if a house is divided against itself, that house will not be able to stand."[4] Sometimes we are like that house, working against ourselves by way of negative thoughts, fear-based decisions, and unproductive words and actions that do not support our own prayers.

Have a vision for your life. Find your purpose through prayer and meditation, and then live the great, grand, and awesome life you were born to live.

Prayer Practice

Several of the prayer practices mentioned in other chapters will help in this particular process. Chapter 30, "Fast and Pray" will be beneficial in drawing out that inner vision that God has put in your heart. Chapter 31, "Know Your Spiritual Gifts," can also support the revelation of your vision.

Whatever God's plan for your life, you have the spiritual gifts to fulfill it. Your role in receiving God's vision for your life is to prepare your mind and heart. This work is done through diligent prayer, meditation, listening from within, and fasting.

If it is possible, set aside a seven-day period of focused prayer and fasting. If you can do this away from your home to avoid distractions, this would be the optimal prayer situation. Find a retreat center that will allow you to remain silent during your stay (see the next chapter). You may set a conscious commitment to fast from negative thinking and solid food for all or part of the seven days, as you desire. But give this life-changing experience all the focus and attention you can possibly arrange, for it will be a time of great transformation for you.

Write out what comes to you in prayer. I have mentioned journaling in many of the prayer practices in this book, and that is because I want to stress that it is important. Journaling is a tool to help you discern and assess the inner revelations that will assist you on your spiritual journey. Besides, in our prayer anchor from Habakkuk, we are told to "write the vision."

It will help to read some of the scriptures where vision is revealed in the Bible. My favorites are Jeremiah 1, Joshua. 1:1–9, and Nehemiah 1 and 2:1–8. Know that anyone who has received God's vision for his or her life, on some level of consciousness, was open to it and prepared to receive it. On the conscious level, there may have been some resistance, such as in Jeremiah's case, and there may have been some fear, such as in Joshua's case, but they did receive what God intended for them. Nehemiah fasted and prayed in response to his desire to make a difference and received the vision to rebuild the city of Jerusalem.

You may have some resistance or fear to overcome. But one thing we learn from reading about Jeremiah, Joshua, and Nehemiah is that what is God given is God driven. "I hereby command you: Be strong and courageous; do not be frightened or dismayed, for the Lord your God is with you wherever you go."[5]

In your prayer time, do the following:

- Acknowledge that the spirit of God in you wants a high quality life for you, "Do not be afraid, little flock, for it is your Father's good pleasure to give you the kingdom."[6] It is your Creator's pleasure to reveal to you what you have been consecrated to be and do.

- Focus your attention on your heart as you imagine God's love for you so incredibly deep and strong that to reveal the vision for your life is God's own act of grace toward you. Your act of love will be to receive it and then set out being it.

- Center yourself in God's presence. (Use your own words in prayer. This is the general idea. The more authentic your words, the clearer will be your revelation.)

- Surrender your life completely to God. *"I surrender myself to you, O God. I lovingly place all that I am before you."*

- Wait in silent meditation. *"In silence, my God, I wait for you. I wait that you may have your own way in me."*

- Ask inwardly that the vision for your life be revealed to you. *"From my heart, the soul of my being, I ask that the divine vision for my life be made known to me with clarity and under grace."*

- Acknowledge the inner resources that God has provided. *"I see myself generously expressing my spiritual gifts under divine guidance and direction to fulfill the divine plan for my life."*

- Spend time consciously bathing yourself with thoughts of gratitude and thanksgiving. *"I am grateful for the divine guidance now being revealed to me as the vision for my life."*

- End your prayer, *"Dear God, Thy will be done in and through me now. Thy will is my will."*

- If you are committed to receiving God's vision for your life, be patient. It may take days, weeks, or even months, but stay with it. Nothing will change your life more drastically for the better than discovering God's vision for your life or some aspect of it and then setting out on the awesome journey to live it.

After doing this great inner work, pay attention to the opportunities that will come to you; they may hold the guidance you seek.

35

A Time to Keep Silence

Prayer Anchor: "For God alone my soul waits
in silence, for my hope is from him."

Psalm 62:5 (NRSV)

I wanted to title this chapter "Know When to Shut Up"; however,
I felt that some people might be turned off by it and miss the great
value of this prayer practice. So I decided to rely on the writer of
Ecclesiastes, who said it in a gentler way that there is "a time to
keep silence, and a time to speak ..."[1]

In the prayer process, there is a time to speak the word of
truth and know it is done. There is a time to speak our powerful
affirmations and trust they are making a change in our consciousness.
There is a time to announce our intentions and our dreams for our
own benefit and the benefit of others. There is a time to offer our
testimonies on the good that God has done in our lives, allowing
others to share in our blessings.

However, there is a time to stop talking so that we may listen.
There is a time to be in communion with God, where we speak no
words, and our purpose is to listen to God within. We go within
so that we may have a conscious experience with God.

In the first chapter of the gospel according to Luke, Zechariah learns the value of knowing when it is time to shut up and listen. Zechariah learns from an angel that his wife, Elizabeth, will bear him a son. Zechariah doubted this; after all, he and his wife were beyond the age they thought it would be possible to bear children. When Zechariah told his doubts to the angel, he suddenly lost his ability to speak.

His speech was restored after his son was born and named John. To be unable to speak for nine months must have been difficult, but it gave Zechariah an opportunity to find an inner connection with God, contemplate his relationship with God, and listen inwardly. It is not surprising that when his speech was restored, he was filled with the Holy Spirit. He also spoke of a prophecy that he had received while he was silent. He announced the coming of a savior for whom his son John would pave the way. Wow! This is the power of silence.

Keeping silent is more than the absence of talking. It is being in communion with the God of our being. In our prayer anchor, the psalmist describes that experience: "For God alone my soul waits in silence, for my hope is from him." All that we could ever hope to manifest comes from God, and the meeting place is within. To gain the full value of an experience with God, we go to a state of mind where we speak no words, and we listen for divine inspiration by listening inwardly. It is a time of surrender. We stop all the outer chatter that fills our daily activities so that we may sharpen our inner listening capability. We go within and find stillness and silence. In an extended time of silence, we may feel moments of sacred communion and be nourished, loved, and supported by the still, small voice of God that can best be heard when we are not talking.

Prayer Practice

This prayer practice is about carving out some time from your busy schedule to give yourself the gift of a silent retreat. Decide on the number of days. If it's your first attempt at silence as a prayer practice, you may want to start with a period of twenty-four hours. After that, you'll want to expand the next period to three, seven, or twelve days—perhaps even more. You can schedule your time of silence as a personal retreat either alone or organize one with members of your spiritual community. Find a quiet retreat center that is conducive to silence. You don't want to have to order your food or talk to the staff or anything.

If you are not able to get away, or just as a maintenance prayer practice between silent retreats, you may intentionally set a full day aside when you can be in silence in your home. Arrange your environment so you won't be interrupted.

- Turn off the phones.

- Don't watch television.

- Do not listen to the radio or read the newspaper.

- Avoid places where people may attempt to engage you in conversation. In fact, plan your day(s) so that you will not have to go out in public to face many distractions.

- Let this be a time of contemplation, prayer, inner reflection, and the enjoyment of being.

- This is a great time for reading inspirational reading material and reading your Bible. Listen for the deeper meaning within whatever you read.

- If possible, get out and enjoy nature. Keeping silence heightens your senses and a simple walk outdoors or capturing a sunrise can have a nourishing impact on your spirit.

In your time of meditation, you may begin by using a favorite scripture(s) throughout the day. Psalm 62:5 captures the essence of what a silent day might incorporate: "For God alone my soul waits in silence, for my hope is from him." If you want to add a little more spiritual power to your silent time, try fasting from solid food and drinking only fresh juices and lots of water. Journaling during this time can also be revealing.

After your day of silence, the answers to questions you did not even know you had may surface. New ideas may come to you with ease. You'll feel relaxed and at peace.

It is helpful to establish a day of silence as a regular prayer practice. When I was going through my ministerial training, I took a day of silence each month. Since those days, I vary my silent retreats, most often taking a silent day once each quarter and then a three- to seven-day retreat once during the year. Once you experience a day of silence (or several days), you'll wonder why you didn't do it sooner.

I sometimes hear from within one of my favorite scriptures in a way that gets my attention. Instead of "Be still, and know that I am God,"[2] I hear "Shut up and know God." It is my soul's way of reminding me it is time for a silent retreat of at least a few days. So that you don't get to the point where your soul delivers such a strong message, I recommend a time of silence carved into your busy schedule.

When you experience extended silence (anything over a few days), take time to transition back into your normal life. You will be working with Spirit on a deep level during your time of silence. An immediate return to lots of busyness and activity may feel harsh to the gentle, peaceful consciousness you've experienced during your silence. Be gentle with yourself on your return.

36

Make a Covenant With God

Prayer Anchor: "Then Jacob made a vow saying, 'If God will be with me, and will keep me in this way that I go, and will give me bread to eat and clothing to wear, so that I come again to my father's house in peace, then the Lord shall be my God, and this stone which I have set up for a pillar, shall be God's house; and of all that you give me I will surely give one tenth to you.'"

Genesis 28:20–22 (NRSV)

As we read the scriptures, we see that in addition to Jacob, God made a covenant with several figures in the Bible, including Noah, Abraham, Isaac, and David. In our prayer anchor, however, we see Jacob being the initiator of the covenant with God. Jacob was not doing anything outside the realm of what God desires from all of us.

A covenant is a binding agreement between two parties. As we view Jacob's covenant we see seven positive decrees upon which he made his vow: he acknowledged God's presence, asked God to guide him, recognized God as the source of what he needed to be sustained, asked for God's help in overcoming his errors of the past, asked God's blessings on his future, affirmed that God would always be present in his life, and committed to put God first in his life and affairs.

Jacob was following God's lead by setting in place the covenant relationship that had already been established with all humankind. "God said, "This is the sign of the covenant that I make between me and you and every living creature that is with you, for all future generations."[1]

God has already made a covenant with you and me. That covenant is the quality of life we have when we live by the spiritual laws our Creator laid out for us. In making a covenant with God, we acknowledge that we are ready and willing to accept this sacred relationship.

Once, when I introduced this idea of making a covenant with God in a workshop, one of the participants firmly objected, saying that God does not make deals. After this, she stood up to leave, apparently thinking she would not finish the workshop.

I asked her to consider that God works in our lives by spiritual principles or spiritual laws. She agreed to this. I pointed out that when we make our covenant, we are saying we commit to working with the spiritual laws that are in place for our use. We agree to do our part so that God working in our lives as divine law can do the rest. When we make our covenant with God, we set an intention to work with God in balance with the law of giving and receiving. We want to receive, so we are willing to give—no deal, just working with the spiritual laws of life rather than against them. We remember that God works through us and a covenant says we will do our part to cooperate in the process.

The woman took her seat and stayed for the rest of the workshop.

When we make a covenant with God, we are not bargaining; rather we are making a conscious commitment to deepen our relationship with God. We acknowledge the method and means to do this is in partnership with God. "With God all things are possible."[2] We are saying that we are ready to take God up on the promise that "it is your Father's good pleasure to give you the kingdom."[3] We're also saying we have knowledge of and accept that "the measure you give will be the measure you get back."[4] We're willing to give more of ourselves and therefore expect to receive more of the goodness life has to offer.

By following whatever guidance God reveals to us during this process, we are blessed beyond just the demonstration. Our relationship with God is strengthened and expanded into a new dimension. Whatever we can do to increase our relationship with God is not bargaining but an opportunity for a new level of spiritual growth.

A general covenant is made in two parts. We follow Jacob's example in part 1. Jacob acknowledged God as his source and asked God for what he wanted. In part 2, he stated what he was willing to do in gratitude and service to God.

Part 1 is easy. Many of us have no difficulty asking God for what we want. However, part 2 is where our work comes in. What are we willing to give back for the blessings we want to receive? Again, it's not a bargain that we make with God; it is living within the spiritual law of giving and receiving. We should remember that God works in and through us by divine law and the gift of grace. God's love is freely given to us as grace; it is up to us to live in ways that honor that love.

Prayer Practice

- For part 1, prayerfully clarify your desires. Write on a sheet of paper "My Covenant With God." You may follow Jacob's format by putting in your own words his first five decrees. (Use your own guidance in drafting your covenant so that it is your own vow and commitment.) This part of the covenant represents your official prayer request. Be as specific as you can, but leave room for Spirit to work. End your request with something that admits you are willing to trust God in this process. Examples are "This or whatever is for my highest good" or "Thy will be done."

- For part 2, prayerfully ask God's guidance on what to give in return for the desire you have stated. Spend time in prayer waiting for divine guidance. Your part will always include serving God in some form; acknowledging God as your source with regular prayer, meditation, and charitable giving of financial blessings.

- Sign your covenant as you would any other agreement and date it. This is important. It represents your sincerity in making a partnership agreement that you intend to follow.

- Read your covenant daily. God will work through you to take care of part 1 while you work on part 2. Stay open to new opportunities and possibilities. God works in wonderfully awesome and sometimes mysterious ways.

The epilogue to Jacob's covenant is that he learned many lessons from which we too may learn. He made his covenant with God at a low point in his life. Through his steady effort to live his part of the covenant, Jacob's life changed for the better. In time, the requests he made in his covenant came to pass. Jacob went on to be a wealthy, well-respected man for the life he lived and for the legacy he left to his offspring.

Part 6

Prayer Practices Simply
for the Joy of Living

37

Make a Joyful Noise

<u>Prayer Anchor</u>: "Make a joyful noise to the
Lord, all the earth. Worship the Lord with gladness;
come into his presence with singing."

Psalm 100:1–2 (NRSV)

Singing has been an important aspect of worship since ancient times. The book of Psalms is a collection of prayers that were mostly expressed through music and sung as part of the worship experience. Today, we continue to sing songs of praise, thanksgiving, celebration, and joy during formal worship services. But this is a spiritual practice that we do not want to overlook as part of our individual prayer experience.

Throughout the scriptures, we see Bible characters singing their prayers, praises, and thanksgiving. Moses sang a victory song after God led Israel out of Egypt, Deborah and Barak sang a song of praise to God after a battle ended in victory for them. David sang many songs of praise and thanksgiving. Mary sang a song of praise to God for conceiving Jesus. Solomon sang songs of love.

The list can go on, but the point is that we have seen singing modeled over thousands of years as prayers and expressions of gratitude to God for answered prayer. Its longevity as a spiritual practice tells us it is a powerful method of praying and celebrating God's presence.

In the scriptures, we find that singing was a natural form of prayer as well as an automatic response to answered prayer. When we sing a song of praise, it is difficult to be sad. When we sing songs that have a positive message, we feel inspired. Singing can help us heal our minds and bodies and find inner strength. Singing helps us to express our joy.

Singing can be a positive method of praying, depending on the words we sing. There are songs, particularly in secular music, that do not affirm the goodness of life, love, peace, honor, and respect for others. Even so, they can have a negative effect on our attitude and therefore block our receptivity to our good.

The spiritual laws of life have no individual respect for people or their circumstance. Negative words in a song activate the law of mind action just as the positive words of a song do. The law of mind action says that we create our outer experiences by the thoughts we hold in our minds. When we sing, we hold thoughts in our minds that will produce the outer experiences we hold when we sing negative or positive words. For this reason, we must watch the songs we sing and the songs that our children sing. Let the words we sing be uplifting. Let the law of mind action work for you to help create the life you desire. Let the words you sing be words that celebrate life and honor God. "Praise the Lord! How good it is to sing praises to our God; for he is gracious and a song of praise is fitting."[1]

When we sing positive, life-affirming words, we magnify their ability to reach deep within us. Singing has such an emotional and soul-stirring range that it can bring us to tears of joy and tears of sadness all in the same song. If we set our minds on singing as a regular spiritual practice, we will discover the benefits are powerful prayers that have the capacity to heal the body, lift the mind, and fill the spirit with joy.

Prayer Practice

Incorporate any one or all three of these practices into your personal prayer time:
- Begin your prayer time with a song.

- Sing a song as your prayer.
- Close your prayer time with a song.

Find songs with words that inspire you, lift your spirit, cause you to smile, invoke laughter, or stir your soul with hope and faith. These are the kinds of songs you want to make a habit of singing. To get a quick lift during the day or infuse a bit of inspiration at just the right moment, sing a song of joy and thanksgiving.

Find songs that say the kinds of words you would say in a prayer. You may consider a hymn that you like and sing it as it is or create your own words to the tune of a familiar hymn. I have a little jingle I sing to myself to the tune of the hymn, "Amazing Grace." It is especially meaningful for me, and I am inspired whenever I sing it.

Every chance you get to sing in a worship service, sing up, sing out, and sing with authority. Remember, you are praying the words of that song, so give it your full voice and the same sincerity you would any prayer you pray. Sing often and sing from your heart.

Since this singing is for you and the God of your being, don't worry about how well you sing or if others will say you can't carry a tune. God cares about your heart and your intention, so make a joyful noise to the Lord as often as you can.

38

Prosperity

Prayer Anchor: "But their delight is in the law of the Lord, and on his law they meditate day and night. They are like trees planted by streams of water, which yield their fruit in its season, and their leaves do not wither. In all that they do, they prosper."

Psalm 1:2–3 (NRSV)

When I was a young girl growing up in Detroit, I did not know that there were spiritual laws governing prosperity. I thought I was to grow up, work hard at a job (that I would hopefully like), claw my way up the ladder of success, and get paid as much as I could in the process.

It was not until my adult years that I heard a minister say that there were laws that governed how we may live a healthy, happy, and prosperous life. Since that time, I have made it my life's mission to learn and live the laws that govern a blessed, well-lived life.

For those of us who *delight in the law of the Lord*, we find joy in living the best God-centered life we can. We are conscious that we have a part to play in our own destiny. We make it our business to read, study, and learn the spiritual laws that govern life. We desire to know them beyond what we get from the Bible, books, preachers, spiritual leaders and teachers. We invest time in prayer and meditation to understand and discern God's will for our lives. We discover that the more we *delight in the law of the Lord*, the more we begin to flourish, grow, and prosper. We read the words, "In all that they do, they prosper," and we want even more to know the laws that govern the great potential we have to prosper.

If we are not experiencing the level of prosperity that feels right to us, our prayer anchor tells us what to do—and it makes the point that the work is ours. The rules of engagement have already been laid out for us as the spiritual laws that govern all spiritual matters. When we learn the rules and live by the laws, we gain access to the rich consciousness that allows us to prosper in all we do. Once we move beyond the consciousness that is trying to get God to give us something, as if it were being withheld, we can begin to accept the abundance that God has already prepared for us through the use and engagement of spiritual principles.

For several years, at my spiritual center in Miami, we held an annual series of lessons on prosperity. One year, in attempting to demonstrate how we all have a built-in millionaire consciousness, I handed out a form titled "You Are God's Millionaire." It was an assessment form asking each person to give a dollar value to our many intangible assets like faith, the love of family members and friends, personal creativity, sense of humor, and so on.

It was a revealing exercise. It demonstrated that we all have so much to be grateful for and that the value of our life is certainly worth more than $1 million dollars. It also confirmed that prosperity is so much more than money. The exercise further proved that most of us are a lot more prosperous than we give ourselves credit for.

Prosperity includes all that is important for us to enjoy a sense of well-being regarding the quality of life that we experience. We are prosperous to the extent that we have the following:

- faith in something larger than ourselves
- health (mind and body)
- peace of mind
- the loving companionship of family and friends
- freedom of self-expression
- positive self-esteem

- dreams, desires, and goals we are working toward
- money to use and enjoy
- a sense of humor

Assess your life to determine the level at which you are experiencing the qualities above. Do you have a strong faith that inspires you to expect good to come your way? What level of health, peace of mind, and harmonious relationships are you experiencing? What level of self-expression and positive self-esteem do you enjoy? Do you have money to meet your needs with enough left over to enjoy the life you desire? Do you laugh a little or a lot?

The extent to which you are satisfied with these areas of your life is the degree to which you are experiencing prosperity. Prosperity is seeing life from a larger view. When we limit prosperity to just money, we are thinking small, and that is a poverty mentality. A poverty mentality places limits on our ability to enjoy the fullness of life.

When we discover that life can be great, grand and awesome, we want to do our part to claim the promises of God. To think prosperity is to think big. It is more than money and things. It is a life of possibility, celebration, hope, and a dynamic consciousness of God. It is creative self-expression, fun, health, joy, peace of mind, compassion, beauty, and much more. If you truly want to prosper in all that you do, think big. You deserve to have all the resources necessary for you to live a blessed and high-quality life as well as all the enjoyments of life that no amount of money can buy—that is prosperity!

Prayer Practices

In your time of prayer, acknowledge God as your source, affirm: "*God is my source of all good.*" This is a truth for the foundation for our prosperity. Say it, write it, sing it, meditate on it, whatever it takes to get this major truth into your thinking and feeling nature. Whenever you pray about prosperity you want to do so from the awareness that all you are, all you can be or have—God is your source.

I invite you to stretch your imagination a bit and do the following exercise. Take five sheets of paper and write across the top of each one "God has provided me with..." On these sheets you will make a list of everything God has provided for you in your life. On the first sheet, list that which is related to your physical body. For example, God has provided me with a heart, lungs, teeth, blood, eyes, ears, mind, etc.

On the second sheet, list key relationships in your life. For example, God has provided me with a spouse, children, friends, (list names) etc.

On the third sheet, list personal qualities and spiritual characteristics such as *kindness, peace*, and *faith.*

On the fourth sheet, list your material possessions, such as a *house,* a *car,* and *furniture.* And on the fifth sheet, list your skills and talents, such as *singing, dancing,* and *writing.*

After you have written these lists (and they should all be long), go back and place a dollar value next to everything you have listed. You will assign a dollar value according to how much you think each listing is worth to you. In other words, how valuable to you is what God has already provided for you?

The point of doing such an exercise is to have you acknowledge that you are already prosperous. Much of what you have listed is so far beyond a dollar value that you would not trade it for any amount of money. Frequently take a look at your long list of what God has already provided for you. Surely God did not provide all those blessings to abandon you now or ever. Use your faith and awareness that God is your source to take you to the next level of enjoying the life that you desire.

True prosperity is lived on a daily basis; it is not just something we pray about when we want something. Someone who feels prosperous enjoys an overall good quality of life, and that can be at any income level. Yes, having large sums of money in our society can certainly expand the ability to buy more "stuff," but we also know that more stuff does not guarantee happiness. Prosperity lends itself to enjoyment of life, harmonious relationships, loyal friendships, peace of mind, and vibrant health. Here's how you may keep your prosperity flowing in all areas of your life on a regular basis:

- Have a daily routine of spiritual practices.

- Be a generous and cheerful giver.

- Affiliate with positive people.

- Take some time to enjoy nature and fresh air.

- Schedule fun time for yourself.

- Maintain harmonious friendships.

- Spend quality time with family.

- Find a place to volunteer your time and talents.

- Take good care of your physical health with exercise and a healthful diet.

- Forgive quickly.

- Keep your thoughts positive.

- Acquire some practical knowledge on money management, investments, and asset protection and put them to work in your affairs.

- Practice love, compassion, honesty, and integrity in your interactions with others.

- Never stop learning.

- Steer your career in the direction of what you love to do.

All these areas can affect your ability to experience life as awesome. Here are some additional ideas to support your ongoing expression of prosperity:

- Be mindful to occasionally wear colors that are uplifting like yellow, pink, or orange, or colors that represent prosperity, like purple, green, red, and deep blue.

- Light a green or purple candle from time to time as a conscious reminder of the light of prosperity that burns in you.

- Sing songs with lyrics that remind you that you are healthy, wealthy, and blessed.

- Keep a gratitude journal with entries of how grateful you are for your prosperity.

- Pray with a prayer partner(s) who supports you in your goals, dreams, and ideas for increased growth and prosperity.

- Keep your home and living environment clean and free from clutter. Make your home your castle.

- Read stories about others who live well and enjoy a healthy life. Remember, what God does once God can do again and again.

39

Dance the Prayer You're Praying

Prayer Anchor: "David danced before
the Lord with all his might;"

2 Samuel 6:14 (NRSV)

I have enjoyed dancing since my teen years. I was never good at it, but I enjoy it, so I kept trying and continue to love it to this day. The freedom to be me was my attraction to dancing. I feel the music and just move. What fun! So several years ago, when I read in the Bible that David danced, I became interested in dancing as a spiritual practice in addition to the fun I had doing it.

I could relate to David's desire to dance. He was celebrating a major accomplishment. The ark of the covenant was finally being returned to Jerusalem. David was filled with joy and could not help but express his gratitude by moving to the music. The scripture says he danced before God. David had done a good thing according to his understanding of God's will. As a leader, he wanted what he believed was best for the people of Israel. The ark of the covenant was their national treasure, and now it was in their possession after one hundred years. Surely this was cause for David to celebrate, and he chose to dance before God.

David wasn't just dancing as an expression of his gratitude; he was having a dance with his Lord. So filled with joy, David could not contain his joy—and so he danced. If you've heard it said that we are the hands and feet of God, could it be that when we dance, God dances in an expression of joy through us?

David praised God with every move, giving thanks with his mind, body, and spirit. The dance was a prayer of jubilation. I rather believe that God enjoyed dancing with or through David by the evidence that afterward David enjoyed a long period of peace and continued prosperity.

Many indigenous cultures enjoy dance as part of their religious and spiritual practice. Many years ago, my daughter became interested in West African dance. I was not very interested in it at the time, but then I discovered that the dances had themes and that the movements were purposeful. Many of the dances were prayers of thanksgiving, celebration, and setting an intention for the desires of the dancer to manifest.

One evening while my daughter was performing in a West African dance recital, she met the man whom she would marry a year later and who would be the father of her children. On that day, I rather think she "danced before God." Her career was intact, and she felt ready to be a mother and was praying that she would meet and marry someone who would also be ready to have children.

One of the many dances she performed that night was a mating dance. In many parts of West Africa, women who are ready for marriage dance with intentional movements and a made-up mind to attract a mate. So they dance and dance and dance. I can say that it worked for my daughter. She and her husband are very happy, and my grandchildren are one of my life's great blessings.

Now it may not be your prayer request to attract a mate, nor is that my point in telling you this story. My point is that the principle of engaging body, mind, and spirit toward a single idea with focus and feeling is a powerful energy to harness in any endeavor. Yes, my daughter did other prayer practices toward her desires, and dancing was just one of them. But I dare say the dancing helped to condition the consciousness to receive the divine response to her prayer, and the first time my son-in-law laid eyes on his future wife she was dancing!

Prayer Practice

Dance your prayer. Whatever kind of dance works for you is fine. Set a mental intention as to what the dance means to and for you. Fix your prayer request in your mind and let your spirit feel the music as you engage your body in motion. Feel free to express who you are. Stretch out of your comfort zone; try bold, purposeful movements. If your prayer is worth consciously expanding the avenues by which your answer may come, then you may be ready to try dancing.

Whatever you are praying for or about may require some courageous actions you have not yet been willing to face. Dancing helps you practice being fearless through the act of trying new movements. Dancing helps the mind, body, and spirit act intentionally and deliver results. Isn't that what we all want our prayers to do—deliver results? When we dance our prayers, we give ourselves permission to let the body move freely and unencumbered so that we shed apprehension. We break out of the box of self-limitation so that we are open to more of the good that we desire.

The gift of engaging your whole being in the prayer helps anchor your intention in mind and facilitate your ability to follow through on any guidance and divine ideas received. As you move, visualize a positive outcome to your desire. You'll be amazed at the feeling of fearless receptivity that will emerge, and you'll be willing to try new things that perhaps you did not consider before.

Find those places where you can express your inner joy through movement. If your spiritual community does not have a dance ministry perhaps you could start one. The principle is the same: engage the mind, body, and spirit in your prayers and expect powerful results.

Dance, dance, dance! Any kind of dance will do. It's a great way to lighten up, have some fun, and exercise the body all at the same time. So pray while you dance, and dance while you pray!

40

'Go Apart and Rest'

Prayer Anchor: "He said to them, 'Come away to a deserted place all by yourselves and rest a while.' For many were coming and going, and they had no leisure even to eat."

Mark 6:31 (NRSV)

You may not think it needs to be said, but it does: take time to rest and relax. This is something I'm sure you already do. However, just as Jesus knew the disciples needed to hear it and then do it, so do many of us need to be reminded of it. We should not take lightly the importance of good self-care through rest and relaxation.

In the story from our prayer anchor, the disciples had been busy. They were doing God's work, had little rest, and took little time to eat or nourish their bodies. Being the teacher that Jesus was, he gave them a lesson in self-care. He wanted them to know the importance of getting away for a while to relax and replenish their spirits. So Jesus took the disciples away to a deserted place so that their rest would not be interrupted and so that they could rest a while.

With the busy lives many of us lead, it is easy to put our time for rest and relaxation off until tomorrow or next month or next year. Answers to the questions we often seek in prayer come to the mind that is free of clutter and busyness. This prayer practice is a wonderful reminder to schedule some uninterrupted time to catch up on your rest and relaxation.

When we let our physical body feel the stressful effects of busyness and long to-do lists, it affects our ability to receive divine guidance, inner wisdom, and mental clarity. When we are exhausted physically, our thought process is not as keen, and our minds are not as sharp. We don't make the best decisions when the body and mind are not at their best.

Our ability to consciously become aware of Spirit in prayer can be impeded by our physical and mental exhaustion. Many years ago, when I was attempting to learn to meditate, I made an important discovery. During the class I was taking to learn meditation, I kept falling asleep. I would try again at home in the evening before going to bed, and the same thing would happen. I did not understand why I could not stay awake because I really wanted to learn to meditate.

I finally told the meditation instructor of my difficulty staying awake. He asked me a few questions about my daily activities, and as I told him what my busy days were like, he interrupted me and said, "Stop, stop, stop. You are falling asleep because you are tired. It's that simple. Get some rest, and try your meditation first thing in the morning in small portions of time, like fifteen to twenty minutes." Well, he was right. I never even realized that my exhaustion was the problem, not my technique.

So whether it's soaking in a relaxing bubble bath, taking a walk on the beach, watching a sunrise or sunset, sitting in your lounge chair, listening to music, reading a book, or just doing nothing, take the time to rest. Do the things that will allow you to relax your mind, body, and spirit.

However, do not think that your vacation is necessarily a time when you will get to rest and relax. If you want rest and relaxation, you will have to plan it. In today's times, traveling can be work. Sometimes we pack so many activities in our travels that when we return home, we are exhausted from our vacation. Schedule some real rest when you are vacationing; balance activity with time to relax.

Also consider a spiritual retreat as an option for rest and renewal. Many retreat centers offer spiritual getaways for a few days up to several weeks. Time for increased prayer and meditation will add to deep relaxation that will nourish and strengthen your spirit.

Prayer Practice

Look for ways that you can combine your relaxation techniques with your prayer practices. For example, if you enjoy watching sunrises or sunsets, plan a time of prayer when you can see the sky. There are times when I have my morning meditation on my patio so that I can watch the morning sun make its grand entrance. Or, if you appreciate a nice bubble bath, take one as you think on God, the beauty of life, gratitude, words of praise, and thanksgiving. The key to getting the most from this prayer practice is to incorporate your prayers into whatever mode of relaxation you prefer and enjoy.

Use some of the other prayer techniques mentioned in this book to enhance the relaxing mood like lighting some candles, putting on some relaxing music, burning incense, or inhaling your favorite essential oils from a diffuser.

Your prayers will be more effective if you take a moment to relax your mind and body. Make relaxation one of your tools for a successful and blessed prayer and meditation experience.

Here is a sample relaxation technique:

- Mentally set aside all your worries, fears, and anxieties.

- Focus your attention on your breathing for a few moments.

- Visualize yourself in a peaceful scene or setting, and slowly say to yourself over and over again, *"Relax."* Do this until you do feel more relaxed.

- Affirm *"I am now relaxed and receptive to experience the presence of God in me. I rest in the spirit of God. I relax in the spirit of God. I am receptive to God expressing in and through me as peace and harmony."*

- As you continue to relax, pray whatever prayer desire is on your heart. Or you may find greater relaxation by reading your favorite scriptures during this time.

- Close your prayer with a statement of relaxation and gratitude, such as *"I now relax and go about the activities of my day. I know that my prayer has been heard and answered with ease and under the graceful hand of God. With gratitude on my heart and in my mind, I relax and let it be. Amen!"*

You will find that if you approach prayer relaxed and worry free, you will enjoy the process of being in communion with God (which is nourishing to the spirit), and divine ideas will find a resting place in your mind.

Again, at least once a year, take a spiritual retreat. It can be a day or two, but longer is better. Give yourself the gift of renewal. Let your spirit be refreshed and nourished by celebrating your spirituality with rest and relaxation. Enjoy!

41

Raise Your Gratitude Quotient

Prayer Anchor: "Give thanks in all circumstances; for this is the will of God in Christ Jesus for you."

1 Thessalonians 5:18 (NRSV)

Some folks seem to be naturally grateful in all circumstances. I was in awe of the attitude of a young man I met years ago, who at the age of twenty-five had been in a car accident leaving him paralyzed and confined to a wheel chair. He always had a smile on his face; he was polite to others; he was grateful for whoever picked him up for church and saw that he was returned home; he loved to sing and always had something fun and funny to say. He was truly a unique example of being grateful in all circumstances.

However, for some of us an attitude of gratitude must be cultivated. Once we begin to let ourselves practice being grateful, it grows on us and in us. We make a discovery about gratitude that we would not otherwise know: Gratitude is magnetic. A grateful heart and mind become a mighty magnet drawing to itself more to be grateful for.

I've kept a gratitude journal for many years. When I finish one, I start another. I list what I am grateful for, and most days I list ten things. Other days I list just a few. Gratitude is a part of my regular prayer practice, and it is a must for anyone who has a commitment to ongoing spiritual growth. We literally raise our gratitude quotient when we develop an attitude to "give thanks in all circumstances." The higher our gratitude quotient, the more magnetized we are for the gifts of health, happiness, joy, peace, love, and prosperity.

The fact that it helps us see ourselves and others in a more compassionate way is another added bonus. When I am grateful as our prayer anchor says, "in all circumstances," I find something to be grateful about in whatever I am facing. If I am in a difference of opinion with someone, I find it easier to forgive myself and them if I focus on finding something to be grateful for in the experience.

An attitude of gratitude can be developed over time if practiced sincerely and on a regular basis. When we pray, remembering to be grateful, we develop gratitude as a habit and thereby establish it as a way of life.

When I was a child, my mother often had to coerce us kids to eat our vegetables at mealtime. She would make us "say grace" over our meal and tell us to be grateful for whatever food was before us. She instructed us to eat what was in front of us even if we didn't like it. She told us it would still nourish our bodies even if we didn't like the taste of it, and for that nourishment we should be grateful. So we ate the carrots, broccoli, string beans, and all the vegetables Mom placed before us, not for the taste, but for the nourishment (and because Mom said so). It was always a great joy on some occasions that for eating all of our vegetables Mom would reward us with dessert. To eat my Mom's peach cobbler or her homemade ice cream was more than worth eating a few carrots and string beans. It was that good! So we learned to eat our carrots, broccoli and whatever Mom placed before us in the hope and expectation that if we expressed our gratitude, something delicious would surely follow. We learned that good things follow the heart-felt expression of gratitude "in all circumstances"—and that includes eating our vegetables.

Prayer Practice

When you pray, start your prayers with a statement of gratitude. For example, *"I am grateful for all God's blessings in my life"* or *"Thank you God for my life, and all the good that continually flows to me for my use and enjoyment"* or *"Gratitude fills my mind and heart."* Make your own statement, but do make gratitude part of your prayer.

Remember how Jesus prayed before raising Lazarus from the dead: "And Jesus looked upward and said, 'Father I thank you for having heard me.'"[1] When we are thankful, even before the outer demonstration, it is an indication of an attitude of gratitude. Praying with gratitude as a theme will help in expanding your consciousness toward greater blessings. You'll discover that you have much more to be grateful for. Your level of inner confidence will allow you to trust that you can overcome whatever experiences come your way. You'll know that you won't face any situation alone. God is love, and we live in that love. "…for it is your Father's good pleasure to give you the kingdom."[2]

End your prayers with statements of gratitude. Also, you may vary your methods by making your whole prayer a series of gratitude statements. Express your heartfelt gratitude for the good you are now demonstrating and the good you expect to demonstrate.

I suggest that if gratitude is an area where you know that you need strengthening, begin right away by listing ten things each day for which you are grateful. Do this for twenty-one days. Nothing is too large or small or insignificant to place on your gratitude list. The important thing is to do it consistently until it becomes second nature to look for the good in your life and in your experiences. This will help to raise your gratitude quotient, and the attitude shift toward thanksgiving will bless your affairs in new and exciting ways.

42

Love and Romance

Prayer Anchor: "And now faith, hope, and love
abide, these three; and the greatest of these is love."

1 Corinthians 13:13 (NRSV)

The desire for intimate love is a natural urge within us. The desire for companionship, friendship, and partnership is our soul's craving for an awareness of our connectedness with our Creator. That soul urge is often imitated by our human relationships with each other. Service, creativity, charity, mercy, and intimate partnerships are all soul urges by which we long to experience and express the love of God. No matter how we express the love of God on life's journey, the important thing is that we do because our soul longs for it.

We are love beings. God created us from love for love. The love of God exists in each one of us. In its natural state, it is always ready to express, grow, and thrive that we might radiate it from one to another. Love is in us and all around us even when we don't see it or feel it. Yet when we speak of love and then add romance to the discussion, the discussion can take as many turns as there are people on the planet.

Though love is something most of us will admit we want and something we already have to some degree, it is one area that is still perplexing to many of us. Our experiences that have shaped our human reactions to love are varied, and our perspectives are enormous: some of us seem to be in love with life; some fall in love easily and quickly; some are afraid to be loved; some worship love's imitations; some have no time for love; some find love in the simple joys of everyday life. So when we talk about love, loving, and being loved, what do we mean? We could study many aspects and types of love, but we would eventually be led back to the soul's hunger for an awareness of our connection with God.

Life is filled with lessons on love, loving, and being loved. But from the spiritual point of view, all love is self-love. The love that many of us spend a lifetime searching for is but our need for the awareness that God is love and that God loves us. "So we have known and believe the love that God has for us. God is love, and those who abide in love abide in God, and God abides in them."[1] Love is God loving in and through us. "No one has ever seen God; if we love one another, God lives in us, and his love is perfected in us."[2]

So our work is to love God, ourselves, and others. The good news is that this is all one in the same life lesson. "'You shall love the Lord your God with all you heart, and with all your soul, and with all your mind.' This is the greatest and first commandment. And a second is like it: 'You shall love your neighbor as yourself.'"[3]

When we claim ourselves to be loving and romantic, we have positive self-love; we love God and we love others. The door to our heart is open with a genuine invitation for opportunities to let God love through us. With this high level of love going on in us, we can say we have a consciousness of love. Love and romance are going on inside us all the time. It is a romance with life itself. To love God, ourselves, life, and others is all one in the same effort and a dynamic expression of true romance. We are romantic for the sake of expressing the pure joy that we exude. This romance causes us to smile a lot. We can laugh at ourselves and at the sometimes amusing twists and turns we find along life's journey. We are romantic because we are love in action. We live the moments of our days filled with an awareness of love's magnificence.

I use our prayer anchor for this chapter on most occasions when I perform a wedding ceremony. Although the apostle Paul reportedly wrote 1 Corinthians 13 to show how we must love others, we can use the same ideals to begin to meet our inward need to know and experience God's love. In the Prayer Practice for this chapter, I make the suggestion that you write 1 Corinthians 13 in your own words with your own personal meaning. Following is an example using the Newly Revised Standard Version (NRSV) of the scripture:

"If I speak in the tongues of mortals and of angels, but do not have love, I am a noisy gong or a clanging cymbal. And if I have prophetic powers, and understand all mysteries and all knowledge, and if I have all faith, so as to remove mountains, but do not have love, I am nothing."[4]

No matter how eloquent the words I speak, no matter my spiritual gifts of seeing into the future and knowing of many things that others do not, no matter how strong my faith, with all these things to my credit, if I do not love myself, I really have nothing at all. If I do not have love in my heart as the foundation for all that I am, there is a void within me that cannot be filled with all my knowledge, faith, and eloquent words. If the door of my heart is closed, I have cut myself off from the goodness of God.

"If I give away all my possessions, and if I hand over my body so that I may boast, but do not have love, I gain nothing."[5]

I will not stray from love's gentle blessings by the glitter of material things. My wealth has its foundation in knowing God's love for me. I gain everything I could ever hope to acquire from the love of God constantly filling my heart, mind, and soul with the consciousness of peace, health, and prosperity.

"Love is patient; love is kind; love is not envious or boastful or arrogant or rude. It does not insist on its own way; it is not irritable or resentful; it does not rejoice in wrongdoing, but rejoices in the truth. It bears all things, believes all things, hopes all things, endures all things."[6]

Others may judge my innocence harshly, believing me to be unwise and unschooled in the ways of the world. But I smile at this assessment, for I know that patience and kindness can harmonize the toughest challenge. I understand what those who judge me do not. My time, talent, and energy are not well spent on qualities of irritability, resentfulness, and rejoicing in the trying times that others face. Love bears the tears and the joys of my days. Love believes the best is always unfolding for me regardless of outer appearances. Love hopes in the face of hopelessness. Love will endure beyond any experience I can ever have. Should my human heart ever feel broken and sad, even then, love will bring me back to itself, whole and perfect.

"Love never ends. But as for prophecies, they will come to an end; as for tongues, they will cease; as for knowledge, it will come to an end. For we know only in part, and we prophesy only in part; but when the complete comes, the partial will come to an end."[7]

There will be many ending places along my life's journey. With all the insight I have into what should be, according to my limited understanding, it is not a sufficient match for the power I gain when I am firmly grounded in God's love. Love has no end. Love is the completeness, the wholeness I searched for in former days. But God's steadfast, everlasting, enduring love is my sufficiency. And now that I know the power of love actively expressing in and through me, I rejoice and celebrate love today and into eternity.

"When I was a child, I spoke like a child, I thought like a child, I reasoned like a child; when I became an adult, I put an end to childish ways. For now we see in a mirror, dimly, but then we will see face to face now I know only in part; then I will know fully, even as I have been fully known."[8]

In my past, I was ignorant of love's power. I spoke, thought, and reasoned that it was not wise to love in all circumstances. I had a list of excuses for not giving myself over to love's magnetic pull. Now, as I live in a state of grace, I am aware that God is the ruler of love, and God's own way of loving is in and through me. I have put aside my former ways of ignorance. I remember in former days when I looked in the mirror, I could not see my own beauty glowing with the radiance of God's love. I searched outside myself to change the picture in the mirror before me. But now, whenever I pass a mirror, I see the love of God looking back at me. I now know what it feels to see love vibrant and alive, face to face. I understand fully that I am one of the many beautiful faces of God's love.

"And now faith, hope, and love abide, these three; and the greatest of these is love."[9]

Yes, I remain faithful. My faith is stronger and deeper than ever before. My faith is in the power of God expressing in and through me now and forever. Yes, I am filled with hope. My hope does not waiver from God's power to heal, bless, and prosper any experience as I turn within to ask, seek, and knock. My hope is in the promise of the goodness of God showing itself forth in my countenance, spirit, and soul. And yet, with all my faith, with all my hope, love stands out in a bold and brilliant image I have for myself. Through all my searching, I came to the realization that God is love and that God is alive and well in my heart. I have discovered the love I have been seeking was always within me. I am love!

Whether your desire is to deepen the love you feel for yourself or to make a harmonious love connection with another, the place to begin your work is within. There are many books that you may read to learn of outer romance techniques. However, in this chapter, I offer you the spiritual principles to not just have love and romance as a possession, but to be the essence of love and romance all your days, from the mind-set that love never ends.

When our soul's urge is toward greater love in our lives, we should consider these principles:

- Our desire for love is the inner thirst to express the love of God from within.

- We can only give what we have, and we receive according to what we give.

- Our outer relationships reflect some aspect of what is going on within us.

- Our overall attitude toward others is reflected in the quality of our relationships.

- Healthy self-love and self-appreciation is a magnet for a healthy relationship.

- The relationship that is most important in shaping the quality of life that we live is the one we have with ourselves.

Our loving Creator has given us the power to choose how love's story will play out in our lives. Isn't that exciting! We get to use the laws of life to create our own love story. A spiritual foundation will enhance your experience of love, whether you choose to be in an intimate relationship with another or choose to enjoy a healthy romance with yourself or desire to have a great romance with life itself. The choice is always yours, and to love is the greatest choice of all.

Prayer Practice

There are four parts to this prayer practice:

- Part 1 of the practice is to develop a greater awareness of God's love within. Work with 1 Corinthians 13 in twenty-one-day increments. When you are reading this scripture, consider it from the perspective of the love between you and God. Take time to write the scripture with your own interpretation, one that has significance to you. After twenty-one days, take a break from it and go to part 2.

- Part 2 is to select one focus area according to your desire: expand your own level of self-love, increase love and romance in your current relationship or marriage, or attract a love relationship.

- Part 3 will help anchor into your consciousness the work you have done up to this point.

- Part 4 is to live your life as the love being you've become.

Here are some general affirmative statements that may be used at any time:

"I am in love with life, and life is in love with me. I am living the great romance of all time—it is with life itself. This great romance is my all sufficiency in all things. I can never lack for love—I am love."

"I find great inner strength, poise, and peace as I express the power of love in me."

"Love guides my way in all that I think say and do."

"I am the expression of divine love and joy-filled romance."

"I love myself."

"I am love in action."

"I am so filled with divine love that I radiate it wherever I go and in all things that I do."

"Every person that comes into the range of my consciousness will be aware of divine life, love, and wisdom as my very essence."

"The love of God expressing in and through me is a drawing power to my right and perfect mate."

"The love of God expressing in and through me heals me now." (You may substitute the word "heals" with prospers, blesses, guides, etc.)

"I am a love magnet."

"God is love; I am love."

"I am loveable, loving, and loved."

Part 1

Morning prayer: Meditate on the words from 1 Corinthians 13 for twenty-one days. Center your thoughts on the scripture sentence by sentence. Contemplate the words as the one being loved by your Creator. As you read the words, feel yourself being loved by God's holy presence. Each morning of the twenty-one days, spend time working with the scripture in ways that allow you to experience being loved and loving. Write out verse by verse what the ideas expressed mean to you. You may use my example from earlier in this chapter. Fill your mind with thoughts of love, peace, harmony, and joy. Let love influence all that you do for the day. Notice opportunities during your day to think, speak, and act from a loving space. Allow this love to affect all your interactions with others.

Evening prayer: Just before bed, read the scripture aloud three times before going to sleep. This will give your subconscious something to work on while you are asleep.

Incorporate some of the other prayer practices discussed in this book along with this prayer. Light a white candle symbolizing God's presence. Then light one pink candle (the color that gives off the energy of love) for the higher expression of love that you desire. Burn incense to enhance the experience. Orange, rose, cinnamon, or orange blossom incense are great for this work.

Part 2

A) To expand your own self-love

Meditate on Psalm 139:1–18 daily for twenty-one days. Contemplate the words line by line in your morning meditation, then read it aloud just before going to sleep at night. Journaling during this process will be helpful. You may uncover areas where you have been blocked. Once these blockages are revealed, they are ripe for healing.

Note: Take extra care with yourself during this time. Be especially good to yourself, more than usual. Make a conscious and intentional effort to spend time pampering and nourishing your spirit.

B) To increase love in your marriage or relationship

If your partner is open to this, read from the Song of Solomon together. Take a chapter each night and read it to each other just before going to sleep at night.

If your partner is not open to reading it with you, then read from the Song of Solomon on your own daily for twenty-one days. First read through it entirely then go back and study those sections you are drawn to.

Note: During this time, also read some books on the subject of putting more romance in your relationship. Reading the scriptures will help build up the inner love and romance consciousness, but you will want to apply the outer romantic experience also.

C) To attract a love relationship

For twenty-one days, read from the Song of Solomon. Read it through in its entirety over several days. Select verses that speak to you and meditate on them before going to sleep at night. Again, this will engage the subconscious mind to get involved and thereby support your desire to attract love into your life.

Note: If you have been without a partner for a long period of time, consider reading other books that will allow you to ready yourself in attitude and outer appearance for an intimate relationship.

Part 3

Go back to 1 Corinthians 13, praying it for another twenty-one days. Write the complete scripture in your own handwriting and read it aloud once daily. Use white paper for self-love, pink if you are already in a relationship, and yellow if you are attracting a relationship. If you sincerely completed part 1 and part 2, your love consciousness has been expanded, and this step will help you anchor love into your essence as you affirm the words in the scripture daily.

Part 4

Go forward in your life being the consciousness of love you have established for yourself. Let your thoughts, words, and actions express the love that you are. You have activated the power of love within. Going forward, let love be your guide. Make it a habit to seek out opportunities to consciously express a loving attitude.

Incorporate other prayer practices in this book along with these ideas:

- Listen to songs about love.
- Sing songs about love.
- Write yourself an occasional love note.
- Use the word *"love"* more often.
- Say *"I love you"* to friends and family often.
- Affirm regularly, *"God loves me"* and *"I am love."*
- Wear love's colors when the occasion arises:
    - red for passion, romance, and attraction,
    - pink for kindness, new feelings of love, and compassion;
    - yellow for attraction, attention, and harmony;
    - orange for friendship, companionship, and positive interaction with like-minded people.

Most importantly, have fun being loving, loved, and lovable. However, if self-love or intimate relationships continue to be a challenging issue for you, seek professional help such as spiritual counseling or therapy—love is worth the extra effort, and so are you!

43

The Power of Blessing

Prayer Anchor: "With it you shall anoint the tent of meeting and the ark of the covenant, and the table and all its utensils, and the lampstand and its utensils, and the altar of incense, and the altar of burnt offering with all its utensils, and the basin with its stand; you shall consecrate them, so that they may be most holy; whatever touches them will become holy."

Exodus 30:26–29 (NRSV)

As a spiritual leader for many years, I have often been asked to bless items—from rings to cars, purses, and wallets to sacred objects, books, houses, business proposals, pens, pets, new jobs, and businesses. Nothing is above or beneath being blessed. I was even asked once to bless a teddy bear.

A young man wanted to give a Valentine's gift of a teddy bear to his adult girlfriend. Apparently, she had never owned a teddy bear as a child, and she grew up under difficult circumstances. He thought a special teddy bear would soothe some of her childhood wounds that she continued to carry. He wanted to be able to tell her that the teddy bear had been especially blessed for her. I don't have to tell you that the teddy bear was a tremendous hit with his girlfriend. I have since been told that she treasured that gift more than any one she received for many years that followed.

Our prayer anchor tells of the Old Testament preparation for worship procedures. Every item to be used in conjunction with worship had to be anointed and blessed. The ancients were very strict about the treatment of what was considered sacred. They were convinced that good, positive energy was important in worship, ritual, and everyday situations. The utensils, the lampstand, the altar, and the basin were all anointed with special oil. Each piece was consecrated to be a blessing in support of the worship experience.

The idea is that objects hold energy that has been conferred on them with high spiritual intention. Our minds are powerful, and as spiritual beings, we have been endowed with the ability to confer a blessing or to pass a blessing on from us.

When we speak words that confer a blessing, no matter what we bless, we set a vibration of increased good into motion by the intention behind those words. Jesus blessed five loaves and two fish, and it increased to the point where more than five thousand people were fed. Our words are powerful, particularly when we give them the intention to uplift, increase, and multiply. At the last supper, Jesus blessed the bread and the wine on the table. Today, people take communion to receive their portion of the blessing Jesus handed out two thousand years ago.

As children, many of us were taught to bless our meal before we ate it. We confer a blessing on the food before we eat it for several reasons. First, with gratitude on our lips, we acknowledge God as the source of all that sustains us. Second, we bless the food that it will provide the nourishing energy to we need to fulfill the dietary requirements for the health and well-being of our mind and body. "Do you not know that you are God's temple and that God's Spirit dwells in you?"[1] We partake of food to provide sustenance for God's temple.

Third, through the blessing of our food, we express our gratitude for the bounty supplied by the earth by way of the fruits, vegetables, and grains as well as any animals sacrificed in preparation for the meal.

Finally, we confer a blessing of thanksgiving on the hands that prepared the food as a representation of our gratitude for the time, love, and willingness of the preparers.

In my mother's house, each child had a fifth item to add to our blessing before the meal. We were required to confer a blessing on the dishwasher. Now back in those days, the dishwasher was not a machine; it was one of us kids. After the meal, one of us would have to wash a sink full of dishes that had fed anywhere from five to ten people, plus the commercial-size pots and pans that my mom used to prepare the meal. So we always closed our meal blessing with "and thank you, God, for blessing the dishwasher."

Blessing is a part of our religious and spiritual culture. We say "God bless you" when someone sneezes. I often hear "Bless your heart" or "Have a blessed day." The fact is that we like to confer a blessing on others as a kind gesture, as an invocation of the multiplying power of our words, or as an expression of gratitude. We may even turn the idea of blessing on ourselves—by blessing where we go, what we do, and what we wear.

We bless the day before us with our morning prayers; we bless our journey to our workplace as we leave our home; and yes, bless the other drivers on the road. Everywhere we go, we bless the path before us.

The clothing we wear may also be blessed. As an example, think for a moment—have you ever had a lucky suit or a lucky dress? You may not have said the words as a blessing, but by believing it was lucky, you blessed it with a title that means extra-special things happen for you when you wear that item of clothing. Is the item really blessed with the ability to help draw good experiences to you? Yes! You are the one who set the mental intention in your mind that it carries good energy, and so it does.

Do you remember the story of Queen Esther? She had a mighty task before her. What did she do before going to the king to make the request of a life-time? "On the third day, when she ended her prayer, she took off the garments in which she had worshiped, and arrayed herself in splendid attire. Then majestically adorned, after invoking the aid of the all-seeing God and Savior, ... She was radiant with perfect beauty, and she looked happy, as if beloved..."[2] She prayed and put on her blessed attire. Who could say no to someone who is majestically adorned after having invoked God's blessing and who glowed with radiant beauty, looking happy? The king could not deny her request. Esther received what she asked for.

Bless the clothing that you wear. Adorn yourself as God's queen or king. Let your inner beauty radiate from you and be reflected in the outer garments you wear. Have you ever noticed how good you feel about yourself when you are well dressed? You radiate confidence and self-esteem. When the prodigal son returned home, the first thing his father said was, "Quickly, bring out a robe—the best one—and put it on him; put a ring on his finger and sandals on his feet."[3] He wanted his son to feel the consciousness of prosperity and well-being. He conferred a blessing on his son by ordering the best outer garments for him.

It has been said that clothes don't make the man, and that is true. But we've heard that the clothing of movie stars and famous people from history can be sold for thousands of dollars at an auction just because that person blessed the clothing by wearing it. You are a child of God, and you have the power to name what you wear as blessed and have it be so. "So out of the ground the Lord God formed every animal of the field and every bird of the air, and brought them to the man to see what he would call them; and whatever the man called every living creature that was its name."[4] Never underestimate the power you have to name the blessing you desire.

From the top of your head to the soles of your feet, you can name all that adorns your body blessed, and expect great blessings to be drawn to you, conforming to your word, which brings me to shoes. I like shoes. Sometimes I shop for them without buying any. I like looking for them and at them. Sometimes when I am shopping for them, they attract my attention. I try them on, and if they feel as good as they look, they are mine. I'm often told that I wear cute shoes. That's because I do. I have set in my mind that I wear cute shoes, and so it is true for me. I bless my shoes. Yes, I bless my shoes. Not because they are cute but because shoes cover my feet and my feet take me where I want to go, to do the things that are mine to do.

The idea of blessing everything is so we develop a consciousness of blessing everything and praising God in all circumstances. This is how we are prayed up all the time. "Let everything that breathes praise the Lord! Praise the Lord!"[5] Whenever you give a blessing, you set a cause in motion for a blessing to be returned to you. If you name something as blessed, it will respond to what you call it, "whatever the man called every living creature that was its name."

Use the power you have to bless everything in all kinds of circumstances. Build into your consciousness the belief that you are always surrounded and enfolded by blessings of all good. In this way, you multiply the good that will come your way.

Prayer Practice

Take every opportunity in your day to confer a blessing. When you come in contact with others, give them a silent greeting: "*God is blessing you now.*" When you pass an accident on the highway, send a blessing to those involved: "*The light and love of God bless you now.*" When a friend comes to mind, send him or her a blessing wherever he or she is. If you thought of that person, he or she may well need a blessing at that particular moment.

Speak words of power and send them forth to bless others and honor the gift that God has given us to name our blessings.

Compose your own spirit-guided blessings. If you are blessing something tangible and it is present, touch it as you are giving the blessing. If you are not able to touch it physically, or if it is an intangible idea, use your power of visualization to bring it to your mind.

The following is a general blessing format you may use: "*In the name and by the power of the Holy Spirit in me, I name you _____.*" Fill in the blank with the blessing you choose. Then define or clarify what the name means to the particular context in which you confer the blessing.

- If you were blessing your favorite business outfit before an important meeting, "*In the name and by the power of the Holy Spirit in me, I name you blessed for success! As you adorn my body this day, you conform to my word and exude wisdom, harmony, peace, and prosperity for overflowing success in all that I experience this day.*"

- If you were blessing the pen by which you expect to sign a major business deal, "*In the name and by the power of God in me, I name you blessed with wisdom! As ink flows from you, so does the confirmation of God's guidance and success.*"

- If you were blessing a new wallet you just purchased, *"In the name and through the power of Christ in me, I name you blessed with money substance! You are the keeper of the rich substance of money supply now pouring in as abundance and flowing out in balanced, wise, and generous proportions."*

- To bless the new job for which you have just been hired, visualize yourself walking up to the new workplace and affirming, *"In the name and through the power of Jesus Christ active in my consciousness now, I name this new job blessed in all ways! In all that is mine to do, my way is blessed with health, happiness, success, and prosperity. The talents and gifts I lovingly share are a blessing to anyone who comes into the range of my consciousness."*

A consciousness that uses the power of blessing all the time, establishes the state of awareness we all deserve and surely desire. Daily practice and a commitment to blessing everything and every experience will help cultivate an attitude that life is good and worthy to blessed. God bless you!

Part 7

Prayer Practices That
Move You Forward for
New Opportunities

44

The Ultimate Prayer of Service

Prayer Anchor: "Jabez called on the God of Israel, saying, 'Oh that you would bless me and enlarge my border, and that your hand might be with me, and that you would keep me from hurt and harm!' And God granted what he asked."

1 Chronicles 4:10 (NRSV)

This scripture tells a short but inspiring story. Jabez, a relatively unknown man in the Bible, makes a sincere and earnest prayer to God—and his prayer is answered. Since discovering this almost hidden story in the scriptures, many people report having been blessed beyond their wildest imaginings after saying this prayer. For this reason the prayer of Jabez is worthy of exploration and study.

A few questions deserve our consideration: what kind of blessing was Jabez asking for? What did he mean by "enlarge my border"? What was Jabez really asking God to do?

The long and short of his story was that Jabez wanted the blessings, benefits, and protections that come with having God use him for a larger purpose. In effect, he asked for a bigger, better life. Jabez asked for a closer relationship with God, one where he would know that God's hand would guide and protect him always. And for this bigger, better life, the closer relationship, the divine protection from hurt and harm, Jabez pledged to accept the responsibility to be of greater service to God.

If you decide to pray this prayer that God granted for Jabez, you would be asking, as he did, for the blessings, benefits and protections that come with having Spirit use you for some larger work, mission or purpose. To pray that your border is expanded is to pray for an expanded consciousness of service to God. When you ask that your border be enlarged, you are asking God to give you greater responsibility in some divinely selected area. When your border is enlarged, opportunities will come your way that will stretch you to a higher level of your potential. The prayer of Jabez clearly asks for God's special blessing. However, the blessing comes with greater responsibility, new opportunities to serve, and tremendous spiritual growth—and all that these entail.

This is one prayer that, when answered, thrusts us into a deeper relationship with God. Our personal answer to the prayer of Jabez will call for a commitment from us to do God's will with whatever is revealed. We will need to surrender our personal will to the larger task that God has for us and those whom we will serve.

Several years ago, I decided to try the prayer of Jabez for twenty-one days. I prayed it three times each day during my chosen period. It was not long after praying this prayer that one of my colleagues asked me to consider running for the regional executive committee of our international association. I had been asked to run the year before and had declined the opportunity. But because I had prayed the prayer of Jabez, I knew that yes was to be my answer.

I was elected and joyfully served on that committee for eight years. I enjoyed the opportunity to be of service to the ministries in our eight-state region. Had it not been for my serving in this capacity, I would not have had the opportunity to meet and interact with so many people, a number of whom I established long-term connections with. The bottom line is that my border (my responsibility in some divinely selected area of service) was indeed enlarged as a result of this powerful prayer.

I said that I had been asked to run for the committee the previous year. What made the difference? I have no doubt that praying this prayer contributed to opening my consciousness and preparing me for new opportunities. My border was expanded;

that translated to a new level of willingness in me to gracefully and joyfully accept greater possibilities to be of service. That is the power of this prayer.

The prayer of Jabez is one that we pray unselfishly. It is a prayer that asks God for more to do that will have meaning and value to others and in the world. When we pray this prayer, our first concern is not for ourselves but the desire for God to use us for something that will make a difference in the lives of others. This is the prayer that invites God to provide us with something awesome that will allow us to give of ourselves in an unselfish mission that will benefit others. The gift is that, no matter what opportunities are presented to us in response to this prayer, God's hand will be there to guide us every step of the way, smoothing out any rough edges. The spiritual growth we will sustain from this close relationship with God will cause us to be blessed in our own life as well.

Work with this prayer when you desire to invite the spirit of God to use you in service to others. You will receive an answer that will allow you to witness the power of an earnest prayer. Your part will be to stay open to the opportunities presented to you and follow the inner guidance that Spirit is sure to reveal. This prayer is often prayed by those who are seeking to know their purpose and have a strong desire to know God's will for their lives. Many have been blessed by this short but powerful prayer and you can expect to be blessed as well. The prayer of Jabez is indeed the ultimate prayer of service.

Prayer Practice

Pray the prayer from 1 Chronicles 4:10. Affirm it with your whole heart and with all the sincerity you feel about serving God. Meditate on the words. Set your intention to pray this prayer daily for as long as it takes to receive your divinely ordered assignment. You may also give yourself a time period in which to pray the prayer, such as twenty-one or forty days. During this process, know that Spirit is working on your behalf, and your job will be to stay open to receive the guidance clearly and then to follow it.

You will notice the movement of Spirit as you affirm this prayer. So stay open to opportunities that come to you. Notice that you will be invited to do things that you had not necessarily desired or considered before. Notice the ideas that come to you. Pay attention to the people you come in contact with and note the kinds of things they say to you and ask you to participate in.

Jabez knew that to serve God was indeed a great blessing. As you pray this short but powerful prayer, great blessings will come on your life and your border will be expanded beyond what you have imagined.

45

Pray for World Peace

Prayer Anchor: "Then the King will say to those at his right hand, `Come, O blessed of my Father, inherit the kingdom prepared for you from the foundation of the world; for I was hungry and you gave me food, I was thirsty and you gave me drink, I was a stranger and you welcomed me, I was naked and you clothed me, I was sick and you visited me, I was in prison and you came to me.' Then the righteous will answer him, `Lord, when did we see thee hungry and feed thee, or thirsty and give thee drink? And when did we see thee a stranger and welcome thee, or naked and clothe thee? And when did we see thee sick or in prison and visit thee?' And the King will answer them, `Truly, I say to you, as you did it to one of the least of these my brethren, you did it to me.'"

Matthew 25:34–40 (RSV)

My mother bore and raised eight children. Growing up, our house was always filled with activity. There seemed to be disagreements all the time between us kids, but my mom wouldn't stand for fighting among us. It didn't matter who started a fight, who passed the first lick, or who said the first provoking word. Both parties involved in the fight were punished because as my mom said, both people should have known better than to try to solve any problem by fighting. She had a no-tolerance rule regarding fighting.

However, I remember one rare occasion when my mom allowed a fight between my sister and me to continue until we had tired ourselves out. At the time, I didn't know why my mom allowed the fight to go on. She stood and watched the whole thing. If we got too close to something that might break, she would move it out of harm's way or nudge us in another direction. But she let us fight to the finish.

There was a part of me that wanted her to stop the fight, not just because I was losing terribly to my older sister, but after a while, I was going through the motions and wasn't as angry about the situation as much when we started; I was just trying to defend myself. After what seemed to be an eternity for me, the one who came in second place, we finally just stopped. My mom had us get cleaned up and then asked us both to sit with her on the sofa. She asked us who won, and my sister proudly acknowledged that she had won. "What did you accomplish by beating on your little sister?" My sister, who was eleven at the time, replied, "I don't know, but I won."

The three of us sat and talked for a time, and finally my mom had us hug and make up. We both were punished for fighting—the winner and the loser. We never fought again. We argued a lot, but we never took a hand to each other again. To this day, we are not just sisters—we are friends. Remembering this story reminds me of the words of Abraham Lincoln: "I destroy my enemies when I make them my friends."

Using my mother's approach to peaceful cohabitation between two parties who disagree on a matter, we can see the following:

- First, they should both know better. When we consider that ninety-five percent of the world's population is reportedly affiliated with a religion and that most religions have a teaching related to the Golden Rule, both parties should indeed know better. "In everything do to others as you would have them do to you."[1]

- When two parties use physical force against each other, what does the winner really gain? My sister succeeded in beating on me, but by her own admission, she did not know what had been accomplished. During the fight, we both lost sight of what we were fighting about. My sister became focused on winning, and I became focused on defending myself. It is the same for relationships where solutions become physical; the issue becomes secondary to the fight. We could ask ourselves, "Does the 'winner' ever really win when the method is violence?" Oftentimes the issue behind the disagreement fades into the focus on "winning" rather than addressing the real issues that seem to divide the two parties.

- Finally, when both parties realize that they will sustain damage of some kind by their own participation in the fight, it just makes sense to find other ways to settle disagreements. My mom had my sister and me sit with her on the sofa. I don't remember what was said, but I remember the feeling of harmony that came over me whenever my mom had us kids sit with her for a talk on the sofa. She was the loving presence that championed peace in our home. I think that if we want peace in our world, some of us will have to champion it into reality.

- If we look deeper into what disturbs our peace, we discover a few cold, sometimes hard, facts about peace in the world, or the seeming lack thereof:

  o If we are not experiencing peace in our home, community, and nation, the individuals involved may be acting and reacting from methods that were used in childhood to solve disagreements. Children fight when they have not yet learned other methods of solving disagreements.

  o If we want to change the outer demonstration of violence in our world, an adult may need to be the loving presence to get the parties talking. I believe some of our disagreements could be harmonized by a talk, sitting on the sofa with a champion for peace and harmony in the midst.

  o The place to start is with ourselves. The more of us who become champions for peace, the more we can affect change in our world—by being it and modeling it.

If we could only arrive at the perspective that we have more in common than what seems to separate us, we would invite the opportunity for a revelation that what we do to one another we do to ourselves. The barriers that appear to separate us are humanly designed illusions based on the erroneous beliefs we hold about others. These would be rectified if we could genuinely see and desire peaceful cohabitation as our hope, fate, and destiny.

As we discover that peace does begin with us, we begin to express it more in our lives. We learn the awe-inspiring lesson that there is a divine and intimate connection between happiness and inner peace. We can then take a stand for peace by choosing it over messages of prejudice, judgment, fear, and ignorance.

We all look forward to the day when we will travel the world and feel safe. We all want to be treated fairly and kindly no matter where we are or where we plan to go. We all want to feel that our loved ones are safe to travel anywhere in the world. "How very good and pleasant it is when kindred live together in unity."[2]

The goal and desire is for all God's creations to live together in harmony and unity. And yet, if ninety-five percent of the world's population claims some affiliation with a religion, why can't we all seem to get along? What has all this "religiosity" gotten us? It is difficult to believe we're all so religious and still treat each other so poorly.

In 2001, the devastating events we now refer to as 9/11 drew acts of charity, compassion, and generosity from around the world. In the summer of 2005, when Hurricane Katrina devastated New Orleans and other Gulf Coast cities through which she passed, the outpouring of compassion was beautiful to witness.

Since that time, when the world has experienced more devastating earthquakes, hurricanes, tsunamis, and tornadoes, we have witnessed the best of humankind through the outpouring of love and support. However, between tragedies, we still have much work to do as the human race and as individuals. "If it is possible, so far as it depends on you, live peaceably with all."[3]

When peace lives in enough hearts as compassion and kindness, we will be proactive in our move toward peace. Then, harmony will be the order of our days. In our times of prayer, we have the power to set in motion thoughts that will build peace, compassion, and unity in our collective consciousness. If we are truly on a spiritual path, peace is on our prayer list.

Prayer Practice

In your time of prayer, light a white candle as the flame of peace shining light into the places where ignorance, prejudice, and injustice appear. Say your prayers of peace, harmony, and joy to the world. Read sacred writings and scriptures that speak of peace on earth, peace among humankind, compassion, and unity. The prayer anchor for this chapter is a powerful scripture that invites compassion into our hearts. Make it a part of your personal prayers to expand your mind toward greater kindness and compassion.

Visualize the planet as a place where the golden rule is lived no matter what our religion, race, nationality, sexual orientation, primary language, geographic location, or anything that seemingly separates us. Pray that we may all not just talk about the golden rule, but that we live it as an example for our children.

Spend time meditating on peace first within and then on the outer. Surround your loved ones, community, city, state, country, and the planet with thoughts of peace, harmony, and unity. Take time to pray for political, business, religious, and world leaders that they are divinely guided in the choices and decisions that they make.

Here is a method you may incorporate into your prayers for world peace. Say the following prayer for each of the seven continents. Light a candle for each continent as you begin to pray for it. You may use a map to identify the continent as you pray, or hold a vision of white light around the planet as you pray for each continent.

Fill in the name of a different continent each time you say this prayer until you have affirmed for all the seven continents on the planet: Africa, Asia, North America, South America, Antarctica, Australia, and Europe. *There is one reality in the universe, and it is the presence of God. The infinite heart and mind of God is perfect peace. There is no place where God is not. The peaceful presence of God is fully present everywhere, all the time, expressed as life, love, and wisdom. Throughout the continent of _____, God's perfect plan of peace and harmony is awakened in the hearts and souls of all living forms. _____, in the name and through the power of the Holy Spirit, I pronounce you the living testimony of peace, prosperity, wisdom, and compassion, now and forever more. The planet is now aglow with your light. Shine on, _____; shine bright! You are the light of the world."*

The following is another prayer I have used in my spiritual community as a congregational prayer, we asked that each person say it daily: "*I prayerfully envision a world, where all people are safe, well, and abundantly supplied with all the material comforts required to maintain and sustain a healthy life; where education, fulfilling work, and creative self-expression are available to all; where planet earth is honored, respected, and appreciated as the home that God has so lavishly provided; where there are adequate amounts of resources that are readily available and accessible for use and enjoyment by all; where a collective consciousness emerges that thrives on divine love, compassion, kindness, and a shared commitment to peace and prosperity for all; where our religious and political leaders operate from spiritual guidance, integrity, divine wisdom, and compassion; where individuals, communities, and nations seek nonviolent solutions to any perceived threats or misunderstandings that could jeopardize the harmony of our oneness; where the central message shared by the world's religions will be a living reality: forgive, love one another, and treat others as we would like to be treated.*"

The sooner we take personal responsibility for peace in our life, the sooner we will be proactive in demonstrating it in our world. "May you be blessed by the LORD, Who made heaven and earth. The heaven, even the heavens, are the LORD's; But the earth He has given to the children of men."[4]

46

Letting Go and Moving On

<u>Prayer Anchor</u>: "The dead man came out, his hands and feet bound with strips of cloth, and his face wrapped in a cloth. Jesus said to them, 'Unbind him, and let him go."

John 11:44 (NRSV)

As we journey through life, we find ourselves in places where we must "unbind" ourselves from what is complete so that we may embrace our next level of growth. Letting go can be a challenging experience depending on what we are faced with releasing, our ability to accept endings, and our willingness to begin anew.

Some of us must really work to let our endings unfold gracefully. The good news is that there is a way to have graceful endings and welcome the fresh new beginnings of our life. If we are willing to draw on our own inner strength and move forward one step at a time, we can face our endings with poise. In this way, new beginnings can be smooth and sometimes exciting.

Like anything else that we face on the journey, it's our perception and views that shape our experiences. Endings and our ability to accept them stem from the many attitudes we hold about ourselves, life, and others. Attempting to hold on to something that is beyond our control and obviously finished is a setup for suffering. The question I have about suffering is, "Why do it?"

Our method of releasing and letting go comes back to love, as many things do. When we love ourselves enough to let go of what is finished, we discover that endings are really a signal that a new beginning is possible and ready to manifest for us. When we really love what is finished, we are able to let it go for its higher purpose to be fulfilled. We may tout that "we like things the way they are" or "we don't want things to end," yet recognize that endings are a necessary part of our growth and spiritual development.

Some endings test our faith in God. Some leave us bitter and angry, and some bring up emotional pain that lasts long enough to devastate our life. This is one reason it is important to have a spiritual philosophy about how life works. If we can think spiritually about letting go, we will not only go through our endings, but we will grow through them.

Our spiritual understanding will help us through an ending that doesn't appear to be in alignment with our perception of good. Our test then is to know and trust that nothing happens outside of divine order and that God is omniscience, the power that is all wisdom and all knowledge. Nothing happens outside the sphere of God's love, power, and wisdom. This may not be an easy concept to embrace when we are in the midst of what feels like a devastating loss. But this is also the reason we do not wait until we experience a loss to develop and work on our own spiritual understanding.

As we face a tough ending, we may do well to ask ourselves the following questions:

- Do I believe the grace of God is a continual presence of divine love in me no matter what I'm experiencing? Even if I am hurting now, can I hold on to my belief that God's love is present in me and in the midst of my situation?

- Do I believe that God's love is a healing presence in my life?

- Do I have faith in God's law of divine order at work in this situation?

- Do I think I know better than God?

- Do I really love myself enough to let go of what is finished rather than holding on to something that represents pain and suffering?

Ask yourself these and other questions to determine your willingness to let go when it is time to move on. When we are receptive to facing what is complete, we will move through our endings with integrity, dignity, and ease while creating the opening for everyone else involved to do the same. If your answers reveal that you are not open to letting go, rather than suffer silently, get some professional help. Talk to a counselor, therapist, or spiritual practitioner to help you sort through your feelings and prepare to move on. In the process of letting go of what is complete, you will discover inner strength that will empower you for the new experiences to come.

Let's face it. When we must let go of what is finished, it doesn't matter whether we are consciously ready to let go. Sometimes we have clues that the end is near and sometimes not. Some endings just happen, with or without our conscious instigation. It may show up as the transition of a loved one, divorce, children leaving home for college, friends moving to another state, being released from a job, and so on. There are times when we must exercise our ability to let go and let God guide us through what comes next.

The writer of Ecclesiastes had these words of wisdom to share: "For everything there is a season, and a time for every matter under heaven."[1] In a long list of occurrences, he lists "A time to seek, and a time to lose; a time to keep, and a time to throw away;"[2] Most of us probably don't like thinking about our need to release as "a time to lose or as a time to throw away," but as a metaphor, it is quite appropriate. To lose or throw away is to cast off from ourselves what is complete, to let go with the knowledge that it is finished, to accept that what we are releasing is no longer ours to hold on to physically and emotionally. I did not include mentally and spiritually because there are some parts of what is being released that we may want to hold on to, and we can find reassurance by holding on. The memories that are pleasant, uplifting, and comforting are always our right and our choice to keep. In our spiritual evolution, whatever contributes to our growth is always with us in consciousness.

What we throw away is our old attachment to what is finished so that we may discover a new connection with what we are releasing. We don't need to release the pleasant memories, only our attachment to the painful ones. Often our inner pain is around the circumstances or experiences provoking the need to let go, such as divorce. The marriage may have been good for many years, so those are the memories we may want to keep. However, the divorce itself may have brought out the worst aspects of the marriage and the people involved. What we want to release then is the pain of the difficult breakup. We want to release the human tendency to get stuck in the ending aspect of what may once have been a good relationship and a beautiful marriage for its season.

While we don't necessarily like knowing it, events have their own course to run, and when they are finished, we must accept the outcome and keep moving forward. Life unfolds in this way, life grows in this way, and life is this way. Our job is to trust that the process of grace is perpetually unfolding in every situation. God has created a divine order to the unfolding of life, and we cooperate with it as we keep moving toward a greater awareness of the power within us to overcome whatever challenges we face. We learn to let go of what is finished and move on. We learn to cast off the pain, keep the best of what is left, and begin to start anew.

In our prayer anchor, we find Jesus bringing Lazarus back from the dead. He spoke words of release by telling people to untie Lazarus, free him from his bondage, and let him go on his way. In this case, what appeared to be the end of Lazarus was not. Endings only initiate change.

Our prayers of release invoke the inner strength to accept change. We speak the words to release ourselves from bondage so that we may grow. There are also times when we must release others from the bondage in our minds. Sometimes we hold on to people, wanting to keep them and the circumstances we enjoyed with them from changing. Yet it may be their time to move in another direction.

Sending my son off to kindergarten was tough. He was excited, but I felt a bit of sadness in the midst of my joy. Our relationship would change, and I did not feel ready for it, but it was time.

The day he packed his belongings and I drove him to college was another tough time. Once again, he was excited, but I felt a bit of sadness in the midst of my joy. Our relationship would change, and I did not feel ready for it, but it was time.

Then I gave my daughter away to be married, and yes, that was tough as well. It was her big day; she was all grown up, beautiful, and excited, but I felt a bit of sadness in the midst in my joy. Our relationship would change, and I did not feel ready for it, but it was time.

These were all lessons in letting go. Sometimes we are not consciously ready to make the changes that are before us, but change is a part of life, and in life, we must learn to let go when it is time. All relationships go through changes. In every change, there is a need to release the way things were, but therein lies the opportunity to create the way things can be. We make it easy on ourselves when we do the releasing part gently and then expect and plan to create great new beginnings.

Prayer Practice

Determine the level of your need to release and move on. The method you choose from what is listed here should be judged by you according to the level of release work you feel you need to do. The level of release work will not be the same for releasing your child to go off to college as it will be for a painful divorce or what you perceive to be the untimely loss of a job that you enjoyed.

Pray the general prayer listed below. The last two sentences of the prayer represent two scripture verses affirmed in the first person: 2 Timothy 1:7 and Philippians 4:13. You may want to write the scriptures in your journal. Next, start with the *Outer releasing activities to support the inner work of letting go*. If deeper work is required (i.e., you are still having difficulty embracing the changes in your life), move to the *Inner methods for letting go and moving on from a relationship that is in transition*.

General Prayer: Take this prayer three times daily for seven days.

"Through the power of God at work in me, I have the strength, wisdom, courage, love, and power to embrace the change that is before me. I place my trust in the unfolding of divine order and know that all is well. I let God guide my way and the way of everyone involved in this change. I let my faith lead me to new found means of joy, peace, happiness, and fulfillment. For God did not give me a spirit of cowardice but rather a spirit of power, love, and self-discipline. I can do all things through Christ who strengthens me."

Outer releasing activities to support the inner work of letting go

There are several things we can do to facilitate the prayer process of release. It is helpful to do some outer releasing along with releasing emotional and mental states of consciousness.

1. This is the time to clean out the closets and drawers that have become cluttered. If you are releasing a relationship, it may be time to take down photos, particularly if the ending came from a painful breakup. Memories can help the healing process, but they can also become obstacles to moving forward. Consciously select which mementos to keep. Some mementos will uplift and help maintain positive, healthy memories, but others may bring up painful times and delay the ability to move on.

2. This is a good time to bring new energy into your home. Consider rearranging the furniture. Bring in some fresh flowers or new plants. We often have a difficult time sleeping during stressful endings, so get new bedding, hang some new pictures in your bedroom, or make other uplifting changes. Make your entire living space a peaceful and inviting place to relax, heal, grow, and prosper.

3. Take care of yourself during times of change and transition.

- Eat healthfully.

- Exercise.

- Maintain your personal hygiene.

- Wear clothing with bright colors.

- Stay in contact with friends, family, and your spiritual community; avoid any tendency to isolate yourself from others.

- If you feel yourself falling into depression, get professional help. We get help to stay healthy and strong, not because we are weak.

- This is not the time to make major life decisions without professional guidance and the friendly advice of at least one close friend or family member who you trust and whose opinion you value. When we are grieving some kind of loss or major life change, our judgment may not be at its best.

- Find a hobby or some fun activity to get involved in. The more you keep your mind busy with pleasant activities, the less time you have to linger in the painful past.

4. Music can help with release as well. Find songs that have uplifting lyrics. In fact, this is a good time to monitor the music you do listen to. Songs that tell of others who are in pain won't help you heal and will most likely extend your time of grief. Remember that you want to be free from holding on to what is finished and whatever is causing you to feel hurt, lonely, abandoned, afraid, or unworthy.

Inner methods for letting go and moving on from a relationship that is in transition

Choose one at a time and move to another as you feel guided.

1. Write a letter to the individual regarding what you need to release. You may need to release anger, fear, thoughts of inadequacy, etc. In the letter, let the person know you have decided to release yourself from the bondage of painful memories and any negative emotions associated with the relationship. After the letter is written, place it in an envelope, read Psalm 23 three times, and place the letter in your Bible for three days. On the third day, tear up the letter into small pieces, place it in its own trash bag, and then throw the bag into your main trash bag.

After a week, if painful thoughts continue, repeat this process to make the release stick in your mind. You'll know when the release is occurring for you; you'll be able to think about the person without the heavy feeling of emotional pain. Be patient with yourself because letting go is a process.

2. Make a list to burn. On a sheet of paper, list all that you desire to release. Only mention names in regard to the painful thoughts, feelings, emotional attachments, and any resentment you hold toward them. Use your own words to address your situation, but here are a few examples to get you started:

- *"I now release all feelings of anger I have toward _____ regarding our divorce."*
- *"I now release all thoughts of revenge and anger I have toward _____ for firing me from _____ company."*

- *"I now unbind _____ (person's name) from any negativity I have been holding toward him (or her). I willingly, easily, and lovingly release him (or her) to the good that awaits him (or her), and now we are both free to embrace our highest good."*

- *"I now set myself free from any bondage to the situation regarding _____. From this point forward, I go freely and easily to enjoy the good that awaits me."*

- *"I now let go of all feelings of regret, guilt, jealousy, and fear toward _____. I am ready to move forward, free to enjoy the good God has in store for me."*

- *"I bless _____ as we both go our separate ways to meet our good."*

When your list is done, read it over once, affirm that you have the strength to let go all that you have listed, and then burn the list. Watch the paper turn to ashes and know that you have made a conscious decision to let go. As the fire dies, affirm that the release in you is complete.

3. Write affirmative statements in your journal. These are positive statements about how you see yourself after you have fully embraced the change and moved on to enjoy your life. Do this daily for twenty-one or forty days. Write your own affirmations, but here are a few examples to get you started. Notice that we are not affirming anything particularly related to the release. That's because you want to see yourself having moved beyond it.

- *"I am a child of God. I am healthy, happy, and blessed in every way. I enjoy the life I am living."*

- *"I feel blessed that I am living a happy, fulfilling life."*

- *"I love myself, and I love the life I am living."*

- *"I feel vibrantly alive and enjoy the people in my life, as they enjoy being with me."*

4. Meditate on Psalm 51:10. It can be recited, prayed, and written to help with inner emotional and mental cleansing. Find an affirmative statement that addresses your prayer desires, or write one of your own and say it often. Here are two variations of the same affirmative statement. I have used it successfully and have recommended it to others many times:

- *"I love myself enough to let go of what is finished and complete. In this way I am a magnet for healthy, happy, and prosperous new beginnings."*

- *"I love myself enough to let go of what is finished and complete. In this way I am a magnet for wonderful new opportunities and glorious new possibilities."*

Finally, set about preparing yourself for new beginnings. If a new beginning is on your horizon, get ready in every way you can for its successful arrival in your life. If you've experienced a job loss, then start getting ready for the new job that is on the way. If your best friend has moved away, plan to meet new friends or set goals to visit the friend who has moved away. You don't have to release the friendship, only the way the friendship used to be.

Remember to always pray for being able to easily let go and joyously move forward. Label all your new beginnings as blessed.

47

Thank God for Friends

Prayer Anchor: "Now when Job's three friends heard of all these troubles that had come upon him, each of them set out from his home. ... They met together to go and console and comfort him. When they saw him from a distance, they did not recognize him, and they raised their voices and wept aloud; they tore their robes and threw dust in the air upon their heads. They sat with him on the ground seven days and seven nights, and no one spoke a word to him, for they saw that his suffering was very great."

Job 2:11–13 (NRSV)

The book of Job opens by explaining how Job was a man who had it all. He had a good relationship with God, lived his life as a God centered man, enjoyed great prosperity, success in the land where he lived, and had a family whom he loved a great deal.

By the time we reach chapter two of Job's story, the man who seemed to have it all experienced great devastation and personal tragedy. Much of his wealth was gone instantly; his children had been killed, and then Job himself was struck with a disfiguring illness—all this on the same day.

Certainly, the book of Job is presented in the Bible so that we may learn from its many lessons. The first lesson from the story that draws my attention is the caliber of friendships that Job had formed. Job's three friends immediately rushed to be by his side. When they first saw Job from a distance, he is so disfigured that they don't seem to recognize him. Not concerned if his illness was contagious or afraid to look at his disfigurement, they proceed to be near Job. This was their first show of support.

Job's friends expressed their grief for Job's situation. They wept aloud, tore their robes, and threw dust on their heads. This was their showing of sympathy for their friend. Next, they did something that demonstrates a high caliber of friendship: they sat with Job in total silence for seven days and seven nights.

There is quite a difference in knowing someone and being a friend to someone. On what was probably one of Job's most difficult days, his three friends demonstrated commitment, loyalty, and a deep concern for his well-being. They did not wait to be asked; they just showed up to be with Job in his time of pain. Friends love us just the way we are; they believe that we will grow through our challenges and will help us to do so when they are able. "A friend loves at all times."[1]

Our lives are rich, full, and blessed when we cultivate friendships where love, respect, integrity, and honesty are the foundation. There is no greater gift to compare with the gift God has given humankind: each other.

We are fashioned after God and designed to love and care for each other. Through prayer and meditation, we develop the pure expression of friendship with God. "Thus the Lord used to speak to Moses face to face, as one speaks to a friend."[2] As our capacity for God-centered friendship unfolds, we enjoy expressing it with others—this is true friendship. As we develop our own friendship with God through living a God-centered life, we become the living expressions of the love we were created to be.

God has given us all the ingredients we need to enjoy, nurture, and grow together in unity and love. We take opportunities to cultivate meaningful relationships, not for what they can do for us, but rather for the joy of expressing the love of God in our heart. The law of giving and receiving handles the love that we will receive based on the love we give to others. That law tells us that the love we give out will be returned to us multiplied. We engage ourselves in harmonious, healthy, God-centered friendships for the gift of sharing God's love with others, and that is love enough. "And the Lord restored the fortunes of Job when he had prayed for his friends; and the Lord gave Job twice as much as he had before."[3] Thank God for friends!

Prayer Practice

Cultivate friendships by being a good friend. "Some friends play at friendship but a true friend sticks closer than one's nearest kin."[4] Pray with and for your friends. Spend time with them expressing the best of who you are. Allow your friends to get to know you, and get to know them. Always hold your friends in high regard. Think, speak, and see truth for and about them. When you pray for them, affirm only the truth about whom and what they are. As you live and model this kind of God-centered friendship, the same caliber of friendship will be returned to you.

You may never need your friends to sit in silence with you for seven days and nights as Job did. However, most of us, at some time in our life, will need and appreciate the care and concern of people we call our friends. A true friend is one you can ask to pray with you and who you should be willing to pray with, too.

So from time to time, ask your friends if there is something you can pray with them about. Let them know if you have a prayer desire that they can hold for you. You may feel that because you are close it goes without saying that you keep each other in prayer, but say it anyway. It is a great reminder of the caliber of friendship you have when you occasionally ask, "May I pray with you about anything in particular? You're always on my prayer list, but I thought I would ask."

"I do not call you servants any longer, because the servant does not know what the master is doing; but I have called you friends, because I have made known to you everything that I have heard from my Father."[5]

The blessing of the meal when you join with friends can be a great opportunity to pray with and for each other. It doesn't have to be long and flowing. Even a brief time of connecting together with God can have a powerful affect on friendships and the prayer that is said together. Join with friends to experience some of the prayer practices in this book and then celebrate your friendships by sharing the powerful results.

48

Pray and Move Your Feet

Prayer Anchor: **"For we walk by faith, not by sight."**

2 Corinthians 5:7 (NRSV)

When my spiritual center bought its new site, it was an avocado grove with about 375 trees on it. We were so grateful for the land on which to construct a new building that we wanted to bless the land and everything on it. We began taking prayer walks each Saturday morning for about six months. (The Miami heat deterred us from taking prayer walks in the summer months.) Anywhere from five to fifteen people would show up dressed in sweats, ready to walk and pray. We would have a specific prayer, ranging from a scripture to some affirmative prayer that had been preselected. We would have a group prayer before beginning the journey, and then we set out walking and praying in single file around the five acres of the property.

We walked for about an hour each time. After the walk, we would gather on the patio, drink lots of water, and then share what we experienced on our walk. It was always a gift to hear how answers had been revealed, fresh new ideas discovered, and gratitude filled the hearts of those who had made a one-hour journey around the property, focusing on God, focusing on good.

We were not surprised when the avocado crop came in that first year more abundant than the property had ever produced. The company that maintained the grove for the previous ten years said to us at harvest time, "I don't know what you people did, but this is the most abundant avocado crop we've ever seen on this property." Our prayers had blessed us, and the land on which we walked and prayed had been abundantly blessed as well. It was indeed a double spiritual gift.

A walk outdoors can be uplifting. The body needs exercise and fresh air; walking outdoors helps clear the mind. When you walk outdoors, you have the opportunity to enjoy God's handiwork in nature. Being outdoors can help us remember that God's power is greater than what we can imagine or do ourselves. Remember when God asked Job the question, "Where were you when I laid the foundation of the earth? … Have you commanded the morning since your days began, and caused the dawn to know its place, …"[1]

There is something about the beauty of nature that humbles us. When we are humble, we are teachable; Spirit will guide us, and our humility prepares us to listen inwardly. "Teach me your way, O Lord, that I may walk in your truth; give me an undivided heart to revere your name."[2]

To pray and walk, or to take a prayer walk, can be a metaphor for what it means to walk by faith and not by sight. When we walk by faith, we move forward; we do not let our thoughts linger in the outer appearance of challenges and difficulties. We move forward with our plans, dreams, and goals in the expectancy of drawing on the power of our faith in God.

When we move our feet, we are in action toward our desires, not held back by our concern over outer circumstances but trusting that each step we take is right, perfect, and in divine order. When we take a prayer walk, we immerse ourselves in the consciousness of praying and moving forward as the powerful movement of Spirit within us and on behalf of that for which we pray.

A moving prayer, an active prayer, also spreads many blessings for what comes into the range of our consciousness as we pray. Just as the trees felt the healing, loving energy of the prayers that we prayed as we walked around the church property, so did the two dogs we encountered week after week. Our neighbor to the north of the property had two large dogs. When we first started walking the perimeter of the property, we would come close to the fence where these two dogs were quietly at rest. For the first few months, whenever we would get close to the fence, they would both begin jumping and barking in a fierce manner. After we had passed by, they would relax and rest again. After several months, these two dogs were as quiet as little lambs as we walked by. They would stand up, look, watch us pass by without barking, and then lie back down. It was as if they could feel the loving prayer energy we were radiating.

Prayer is powerful when we are still as well as when we are moving. This particular prayer process invites you to set a conscious time of prayer while actively moving your feet—walking, jogging, running. Most of us are familiar with praying and being still, but to walk and consciously pray is a bit different. "The Lord appeared to Abram and said to him, 'I am God Almighty; walk before me, and be blameless.'"[3]

As you take steps on your outer journey, while having an inner prayerful experience, know that you are on your right path toward the realization of your desires.

Prayer Practice

Walk and pray. The idea is to set your prayerful thoughts toward your desire and move your feet. Do this outdoors if possible so that you get the added blessing of engaging nature on your journey. You set your own intention, make it a faith walk, a love walk, a peace walk, a joy walk, a prosperity walk; you name the kind of thoughts you will hold in your consciousness as you move your feet.

Take your walk with the realization that God is within you as you make your prayerful journey. Set your intention to "walk blameless before God." This says that your thoughts will be without error and focused on truth, faith, life, love, and wisdom. Decide that you will be open to the divine ideas that are sure to be revealed to you on your journey. Expect possibilities to be made known to you during this time. Walk with the truth that "with God, all things are possible," the expectation that your faith in God brings answers and divine blessings.

You may decide to use a particular affirmation, scripture, or prayer that focuses on your faith in God. If so, print it on an index card and carry it with you or commit it to memory. Decide on what prayer best suits you, or let your prayers flow from your heart. You may even consider letting Spirit put a prayer in your heart as you begin your walk. The important thing is to be open and focus your attention on God, life, truth, and divine ideas and then move.

Find a place to walk where you will not be disturbed by heavy traffic. You may find a place that has a walking path that has been intricately designed, such as a labyrinth. Any place with beautiful scenery such as a park or walking trail near a lake will be especially nourishing to your spirit as you pray, and move your feet.

49

Pray up the Life You Desire

Prayer Anchor: "Do not be conformed to this world, but be transformed by the renewing of your minds, so that you may discern what is the will of God—what is good and acceptable and perfect."

Romans 12:2 (NRSV)

The theme that runs through this book is that we can make what we think, say, and do a prayerful experience. The beauty of this principle is that through prayer, we get to create the life we desire. When we pray, we participate in unfolding the life we want, the person we want to be, and the things we want to do.

Each day we face the thoughts, words, and deeds that we have manifested. We planted them in our hearts and minds as seeds in earlier times. We allowed them to grow by giving them space to take root in our mind. There they were nourished with the inner beliefs we held toward them. And now we face them—good, not so good, or indifferent. The good news is that we may now consciously use this same process to create what we choose to face tomorrow and beyond.

Our prayer anchor for this chapter gives a compelling message on how we are to use our thoughts, words, and prayer power to create the life we desire. It lets us know we should never just accept the way things appear as the way they must always be. We are not to be conformed to the small plans that others have adopted for themselves. When we pray, we renew our minds and prepare for our good.

Life is huge, expansive, and grand, and it should be experienced in a major way. The language of the scripture is strong: "Do not be conformed to this world." Sometimes it takes a firm stance to understand just how important words of truth are to our health, prosperity, and well-being. We are given this message in a forceful way because it will require from most of us a great deal of practice, training, and study to follow these powerful instructions that have the capacity to change our lives for the better.

We are accustomed to believing circumstances as we see with our eyes. We like to check the facts and figures of what has already been done. We like knowing the results of the past before we make a decision to move forward. We love to engage the opinions of others. Certainly there is a time and place for this, but our scripture tells us not to conform to all the data gathering we do in conjunction with moving our lives forward. We are to follow a path that will lead us to the will of God—what is good and acceptable and perfect. And anyone reading a book on prayer is certainly seeking this path.

The challenge for many of us, however, is that we must overcome our early childhood conditioning. We were taught from childhood to conform. The child who has a difficult time in the educational system is the one who has his or her own ideas. Generally, children are not taught to have their own ideas or to think creatively. Life is easier for the child who learns to conform early in life. Children do not like being singled out for being "different" from their peers. This early childhood conformity robs young people of the creative possibilities that the mind was designed to express. Our capacity to dream, envision, create, and take on the seemingly impossible goes largely unused unless we heed the words of our prayer anchor. Through prayer, we position ourselves to move beyond the conformed ways the world thinks so that we may renew our minds in the life, love, and wisdom of God.

Conformity can be detrimental—we find ourselves doing what has already been done and missing out on new possibilities. We should ask ourselves, "Does this way of thinking honor my God-given gifts of imagination, faith, power, wisdom, strength, and zeal?" Many of us are content with a few trinkets that imitate happiness rather than claiming the true happiness we all deserve. God has given us a mind with which we may make choices and decisions based on our individual expression of wisdom and creativity. When we get out of the conforming mind-set, we are ready to be transformed.

But what does it mean to be transformed by the renewing of our minds? Our lives can be changed and wholly uplifted by understanding and using the power of thought consciously and intentionally. God has given us the ability to think big or small. And what we dwell on in thought, with feeling, shapes our experience. So when we think our thoughts, we are making a personal investment in what will show up as our experience. Transformation then becomes the revelation and catalyst for the acceptance that we deserve to enjoy a high-quality life and that there is path to attain it.

So the plan is this: invest your thoughts moment by moment, day after day in the life you desire to live. Your ongoing thoughts are the prayers that lead to the life you will get to live. When you pray up your life, you are using your thoughts and prayers to invest in the quality of life you want for yourself. The life you'll live in the future is being crafted today by the conscious thoughts and prayers you hold in your mind. Consciously choose thoughts that will bring returns of happiness and great joy.

Make a commitment today to use the power of your thoughts with intention and purpose toward living the best life God created you to live. The will of God, which is good, acceptable, and perfect, will surely be the result you experience.

When we think intentionally, we are setting in motion the law of cause and effect, which will return results to us as we have initiated. So we make our thoughts loving, our words sweet, and our actions kind. This transformation we seek in the outer first begins with the decision to not conform our way of thinking with negative thinking around us. We practice and train ourselves to use God's gift of inner strength to override the human tendency toward negative, self-defeating, anxious, worried thoughts. We reach for godly thoughts at every turn, in all situations and in every circumstance.

The more we focus our thoughts and words on what is positive, uplifting, life affirming, healthy, and prospering, then we have created our lives as a living prayer, and we can say we are prayed up. In this way, we embrace the words of the apostle Paul: "Rejoice always, pray without ceasing."[1]

Prayer Practice

Read the prayer anchor for this chapter daily for twenty-one days. Become sensitive to your daily thoughts, words, and actions. Notice where you are conforming to the crowd rather than listening and following your own inner guidance. Reading the scripture will help you to stay conscious of your mental decisions.

For each of the twenty-one days, pray and meditate on any of these affirmative prayers or construct your own. This is the work that will help to transform your mind and your way of thinking.

- *"Through the power of the Holy Spirit in me, I transform my every thought to surrender to the will of God for my life."*

- *"I use my God-given power of thought to think of life, love, wisdom, peace, joy, health, and prosperity."*

- *"Divine love, active in me, fills my mind, moment by moment, day by day, with thoughts of peace, harmony, health, and prosperity."*

- *"Through the grace of God, active in my mind, my every thought is toward peace."* (Say this prayer seven times, each time inserting a new word in place of peace such as *joy, health, wholeness, love, life,* or *divine order*).

Use your days to think on words that are positive, uplifting, and life affirming. Stay prayed up. Pray often, pray sincerely, and practice what you pray. In this way, you *Pray Up Your Life!*

50

Let Your Light Shine

Prayer Anchor: "Then God said, 'Let there be light'
and there was light. And God saw that the light was good;
and God separated the light from the darkness."

Genesis 1:3-4 (NRSV)

According to the allegorical account of the creation in the first chapter of Genesis, on the first day, God created light. God spoke it into being, and there it was. We can understand why light would come first because, according to the story, there was chaos and darkness. So the light was made to dispel the chaos and shed awareness into the mystery called darkness.

As I write these words, I am watching a most gorgeous sunset from an airplane headed to Miami. As the sun sets, it disappears from my eyesight but not my insight. The light radiating from it shows colors of orange, yellow, a touch of red, and what seems to be peach. Its beauty is indescribable. And although the sun is not mentioned until the fourth day of creation, my sense is that the light created on the first day was like the beauty I now see glowing from this sunset before me. That first appearance of light on the first day of creation made its grand entrance with elegance and grace. Perhaps its purpose was to set the stage for all good things to follow.

I remember an experience I had many years ago that was so profound I can remember it vividly. I was driving home from work one day, and the sunset caught my eyes. It was so beautiful that I pulled off the road and parked so that I could watch the awesome sight in the sky. I sat there for probably fifteen to twenty minutes. It was such a beautiful view that it brought tears to my eyes. I had a sense that I was one with the gorgeous light show in the sky. I remember thinking: *Surely God who created such an awesome vision would want someone to notice it. Surely God would find pleasure if we, God's children, would stop for a few moments from our busy schedule to take in the beauty of the sunrises and sunsets so elegantly displayed day after day.*

When I was able to compose myself and get back on the road, I went home deeply affected by the experience in a way I could not put into words. I wanted to tell someone, anyone, everyone but the thought of trying to describe the profound experience would have demeaned it. There was no way to describe something that outstanding and give it a fair description. It was beyond words.

Now, whenever I watch a sunset or a sunrise, I sense a connection with the largeness of life itself. I feel small compared to the sun, and at the same time, I feel larger than I've believed myself to be. It is difficult to witness a sunrise or a sunset and feel alone and hopeless. "God saw that the light was good," and when I see the carefully sketched beams of light stretching across the sky, I think, *Yes, God is right—the light is good.*

In the gospel according to Matthew, it is reported that we are connected to the light and to each other. "You are the light of the world. A city built on a hill cannot be hid. No one after lighting a lamp puts it under the bushel basket, but on the lampstand, and it gives light to all in the house. In the same way, let your light shine before others, so that they may see your good works and give glory to your Father in heaven."[1]

As the light of the world, we have the potential to glow and shine as magnificent expressions of God. The light of God that shines in and through us will be an inspiration to all who witness the light that we are. The light is not ours to harbor or keep from others or from the world. The scripture tells us that we are to share our inner light with others. We have no right to deny the world our light. To not let our light shine would be like God creating a gorgeous sunrise and hiding the rays of light that naturally shine from the sun or like hiding the sun itself. We would be missing the convergence of flawless beauty and grace stretched elegantly across the sky into what seems to be eternity. It is unfathomable to think our Creator would hide such an extraordinary presentation.

And so it is with us. We, too, are the light of God created to express magnificence. We are charged with the privilege and the responsibility to let that light shine in and through us. The light of God expresses in us as streams of consciousness beaming truth, life, love, and wisdom on earth as it is in heaven. In one radiant stream of light, there is pure potential for total illumination for all creation. We have the capacity to claim our illumined consciousness by turning up our inner light. As we do, we extend our reach to places where truth and grace are needed—first within ourselves and then to others. We let our light shine on the path within and before us, illuminating the way by which we can see grander potential in ourselves and all humankind.

Joy unfolds as the inner light reveals that our Creator generously poured the potential for full illumination into each one of us. We feel the power behind the words "Let there be light" as a flicker of the holy flame within. As the inner light grows brighter, we harness the power to heal, inspire, encourage, lift, bless, and love beyond what we can ever imagine. Sometimes our inner light shines so bright that it becomes the light by which others may see the way of hope, possibility, faith, and renewed strength. And then, in a moment revealed through pure enlightenment, we will join the light that we are with the lights of our fellow travelers on life's journey, igniting a convergence of awakened potential emerging as unlimited possibilities of peace and prosperity for all humankind. The light of divine love shall at long last be felt in every human heart shedding its brilliance across the soul of all God's creations. In this way, our true magnificence is unveiled, and we will be the living expression of what we were created to be from the first day of creation: the light of the world.

Prayer Practice

Watch a sunrise or sunset. Set an appointment to sit and watch the horizon, beginning the hour before the sunrise or just before the sun sets so you get to experience the entire event. You're not worshiping the sun, but you are enjoying the beauty of what God has created. Remind yourself that the same kind of awesome beauty is within you.

Use the light as a visual in your time of prayer. Let the light illumine your mind and heart, putting you in tune with the goodness of God and the many ways good shows up in your life. This is a great time to burn a candle in the outer as you are working with your inner light.

To develop a consciousness of healing, spiritual understanding and divine guidance, use the following prayer practice:

- Visualize your body surrounded by a white light.

- Imagine that you are tracing the outer form of your body with this light. Start at the top of your head going down the left side of your body, under your feet, up the right side of your body, and back to the top of your head. Make this journey of light three times around your body.

- With each journey, affirm over and over, *"Let there be light."*

- Continuing to visualize, bring the light from the top of your head down into your heart space, just left of the center of your body. Hold the light in your heart space for a few moments in silence.

- Affirm, *"The light of God shines in and through me."*

- If there is any particular prayer that you are working with, shine the light on your desire by thinking on your prayer while continuing to hold the light on your heart space.

- Sit in silence holding the light and your attention in your heart. Breathe deeply and fully; consciously inhale and exhale.

- When you are ready to end your prayer affirm, *"I am the light of my inner world"* followed by, *"I am a bright light shining in my outer world."*

- When you feel a sense of peace regarding the experience, express your gratitude and say, *Amen!*

You may use this same prayer practice for specific prayer desires; just change the color of the light as follows:

- For healing, visualize a green or white light.

- For love, visualize a pink light.

- For wisdom and creativity, visualize a yellow light.

- For faith and peace of mind, visualize a blue light.

- For prosperity and spiritual power, visualize a purple light.

Dear friend, wherever you go and in all things that you do, let the magnificence of your inner light shine, shine, shine! You are the light of the world!

Closing Prayer

Beloved of God,

As you grow in your conscious awareness of God's presence ever
active in you,
May you dwell under grace in the secret place of the Most High.
May you abide safely in the shadow of the Almighty.
May all that you think, say, and do be anchored in divine wisdom.
May the cloak of royalty rest gently on your shoulders, as you
prosper in every way and
in accordance with every good desire.
With each prayer that you pray and live,
know that you are creating the life that you so earnestly desire,
and so richly deserve.

Abundant blessings always,
Charline

Acknowledgements

I have dreamed of writing a "public" gratitude page since I was a little girl. I dreamed that one day I would write a book that would be published, and I would celebrate the accomplishment by writing my acknowledgement page as my very own gratitude list. I have kept a gratitude journal for many years, so the writing of this page was the easiest page to write in the entire book.

Abraham Lincoln once said, "All that I am I owe to my mother." I could say that too. My mother had the kind of faith that I've seen in only a few people in my life. She went through times of challenge that most people could never even imagine, yet her faith in God never waivered and she always believed that, no matter what the experience, a prayer would surely help. She continues to be an inspiration to me long after her transition. However, there have been many others, in addition to my mother, who have added to the person I continually aspire to become.

My two children are my angels from God. They have given me the gift of discovering love. It is my greatest joy to have them call me Mom. I am grateful to my brothers and sisters who have each in their own way contributed to my soul growth and development.

I am grateful for the life lessons inspired by the memory of my late husband, Carlos, whose transition sparked the motivation for this book.

For all my spiritual teachers who encouraged me to keep moving forward no matter what. There have been many people, but a few I must mention: Reverend Ruth Mosley and the late Reverends Maurice Williams, David Williamson, and Jack Boland.

I am so thankful to my colleagues who motivate me by the awesome example of truth by which they live; again there are many, but I must mention a few: Diana McDaniel, Nancy Norman, James Trapp, Robert Marshall, and Argentina Glasgow.

My heartfelt thank-you for my review, editorial, and technical team who freely gave of their time and talents: Tiffany Manuel, Diana McDaniel, Nancy Norman, Karen Morris, Karen Kuebler, Mamie Spring, Akilah Malcolm, and to the publisher.

Much gratitude goes to my prayer partners on this project. Their prayers helped to pull this book into form: Pinky Sands, Chyrl Ann Forbes, Rosalind Malcolm, Seereah Beckett, Shauna Edwards, and Jean Gulliver.

And last, but certainly not least, my heart is filled with love and gratitude for the entire congregation of Unity Center of Miami. The radiating center of love that we have been together helped make writing this book a healing and uplifting experience. I will always be grateful.

About The Author

Charline E. Manuel is an inspirational teacher, spiritual leader, lecturer, and author. She is frequently asked to speak on the subjects of personal and spiritual growth, prayer, goal setting, journaling, and metaphysical studies. Ordained as a Unity minister by Unity School of Christianity in 1995. She has encouraged thousands of people through her Sunday messages, lectures, seminars, workshops, and international mission initiatives. With a message of faith, hope and well-being for all, she assists men, women, and children in the transformation of their lives by focusing on practical approaches to a positive way of living. In addition to *Pray Up Your Life,* she is author of the *Pray Up Your Life Companion Workbook*. Her latest book is titled *The Metaphysics of Shoes*. www.prayupyourlife.com or www.charlineemanuel.com

Scripture Notes

KJV King James Version; NKJV New King James Version;
NRSV New Revised Standard Version
RSV Revised Standard Version

Chapter 1 – First Things First

1. Matthew. 6:33 (NKJV)

2. Proverbs 3:5-6 (NKJV)

3. Genesis 1:31 (NKJV)

4. Luke 17:21 (NKJV)

5. Exodus 3:13–14 (KJV)

Chapter 4 – Be Persistent—Pray Until Something Happens

1. Luke 18:1 (NRSV)

2. John 5:17 (NRSV)

Chapter 7 – Prayer Partners

1. Matthew 17:2 (NRSV)

Chapter 9 – Bless Your Business

1. 1 Chronicles 29:10–11 (NKJV)

2. 1 Chronicles 29:12 (NKJV)

3. 1 Chronicles 29:13 (NKJV)

4. 1 Chronicles 29:16 (NKJV)

5. 1 Chronicles 29:21 (NKJV)

Chapter 36 – Make a Covenant With God

1. Genesis 9:12 (NRSV)
2. Matthew 19:26 (NKJV)
3. Luke 12:32 (NKJV)
4. Luke 6:38 (NRSV)

Chapter 37 – Make a Joyful Noise

1. Psalm 147:1 (NRSV)

Chapter 41 – Raise Your Gratitude Quotient

1. John 11:41 (NRSV)
2. Luke 12:32 (NKJV)

Chapter 42 – Love and Romance

1. 1 John 4:16 (NRSV)
2. 1 John 4:12 (NRSV)
3. Matthew 22:37–39 (NRSV)
4. 1 Corinthians 13:1–2 (NRSV)
5. 1 Corinthians 13:3 (NRSV)
6. 1 Corinthians 13:4–7 (NRSV)
7. 1 Corinthians 13:8–10 (NRSV)
8. 1 Corinthians 13:11–12 (NRSV)
9. 1 Corinthians 13:13 (NRSV)

Chapter 43 – The Power of Blessing

1. 1 Corinthians 3:16 (NRSV)
2. Addition to Esther 15:1–5 (RSV)

Chapter 48 – Pray and Move Your Feet

1. Job 38:4, 12 (NRSV)

2. Psalm 86:11 (NRSV)

3. Genesis 17:1 (NRSV)

Chapter 49 – Pray up the Life You Desire

1. 1 Thessalonians 5:16–17(NRSV)

Chapter 50 – Let Your Light Shine

1. Matthew 5:14–16 (NRSV)

Bibliography

Allen, J. (1997). *The Wisdom of James Allen, Five Books in One*. Arbuckle, California: Radiant Summit Books.

Bourgeault, C. (2006). *Chanting the Psalms*. Boston, Massachusetts: New Seeds Books.

Cady, H. E. *Lessons In Truth*. Unity Village, MO: Unity School of Christianity.

Cunningham, S. (2004). *Cunningham's Encyclopedia of Crystal, Gem & Metal Magic*. St. Paul, Minnesota: Llewellyn Publications.

Fillmore, C. (1936). *Prosperity*. Unity Village, MO: Unity Books.

Fillmore, C. (1959). *The Revealing Word*. Unity Village, Missouri: Unity Books.

Hasbrouck, H. (1984). *Handbook of Positive Prayer*. Unity Village, MO: Unity Books.

Hay, Louise. (1996). *Gratitude - A Way of Life*. Carlsbad, Californai: Hay House, Inc.

Kingma, D. R. (2006). *101 ways to Have True Love in Your Life*. Boston, MA: Conari Press.

Marcelis, N. (2001). *Home Sanctuary*. Chicago, IL: Contemporary Books.

Ponder, C. (1977). *The Millionaire Moses*. Camarillo, California: DeVorss Publications.

Ponder, C. (rev. ed., 1987). *The Millionaires of Genesis*. Marina del Rey, California: DeVORSS & COMPANY.

Robyn, K. L. (2001). *Spiritual Housecleaning.* Oakland, CA: New Harbinger Publications, Inc.

Spear, W. (1995). *Feng Shui Made Easy.* New York, NY: HarperCollins Publishers.

Index